Learning to Code

An Invitation to
Computer Science through
the Art and Patterns
of Nature

Lynx Edition

David D. Thornburg, PhD

Constructing Modern Knowlege Press

Published by Constructing Modern Knowledge Press, Torrance, CA USA

cmkpress.com

This and other Constructing Modern Knowledge Press books may be purchased at cmkpress.com. Volume and education discounts are available.

ISBN

Paperback: 978-1-955604-02-4

Hardcover: 978-1-955604-03-1

COM051000 COMPUTERS / Programming / General

EDU039000 EDUCATION / Computers & Technology

EDU029010 EDUCATION / Teaching Methods & Materials / Mathematics

Cover: Yvonne Martinez

Layout: Sylvia Martinez

The flowers appear on the earth;
the time of the singing of the birds is come,
and the voice of the turtle is heard in our land...

The Song of Solomon 2:1

This book is dedicated to the memory of Seymour Papert, a friend and colleague going back to the early 1970s, when he got me hooked on the idea that children could transform their understanding of mathematical ideas through learning to create their own programs.

Contents

Preface

This is a book that deals with three topics—graphic art, geometry, and computer programming—as though they were braided together into one cord. At any point in this book, one thread may be more visible than the others, yet I have endeavored to interrelate them in a coherent, meaningful way.

I don't expect that readers of this book are expert artists, mathematicians, or computer programmers. I hope, however, that if readers are interested in at least one of these topics, the text will help them make enjoyable discoveries in the other two fields.

For many reasons, a version of the computer language Logo has been chosen as the programming environment for this book. Logo is an exceptionally powerful language whose syntax allows it to be learned easily by people who have had no previous experience with computers. Seymour Papert's *Mindstorms: Children, Computers and Powerful Ideas* describes both the motivation behind the language and its enthusiastic reception by neophyte computer users of all ages.

The version chosen for this book is called Lynx, a cloud-based implementation that can be accessed online at lynxcoding.club and can be used on any device that has a web browser—computers, Chromebooks, tablets, and even smartphones! This means that Lynx can be used by literally billions of people worldwide. To get started, sign up for the 30-day trial version, and then you can upgrade to the permanent version for a very low price. All the features we'll use are available in all versions.

Since Lynx is a version of Logo, why not use that name? Well, the animal called the Lynx has the same name in both English and French. Since Lynx was developed in Canada, a bilingual country, this name is a nice reminder of its place of origin.

Much of the excitement surrounding Lynx is a result of its incorporation of a beautifully simple and powerful graphics environment. Pictures are created on the display screen by giving instructions to an imaginary "turtle," which draws lines as it moves along. These instructions take the form of a descriptive procedure of the object being drawn. As this book is devoted primarily to "turtle graphics," it is perhaps beneficial to compare the turtle's characteristics to those of conventional coordinate geometry.

In familiar (Cartesian) planar geometry, the location of a point in a plane is specified by its coordinates (usually denoted by the letters x and y). The x coordinate measures the point's position from a vertical reference line, and the y coordinate measures the point's distance above (or below) a horizontal reference line.

Another way of describing the properties of a point is to specify its orientation as well as its x and y coordinates. There are several reasons why this additional piece of information is valuable. First, it allows simple representation of a graphic object through a procedure that, when followed, will generate the object. For example, if our point (which we will call the turtle) is pointing straight up, we can describe a 50 unit square by the following set of instructions:

```
forward 50 (units)
right 90 (degrees)
forward 50
right 90
forward 50
right 90
forward 50
right 90
```

These commands produce this image.

(Don't worry about the details, we'll get to that later.) Aside from the utility of this type of representation in developing an intuition for geometry, an even more compelling reason to be interested in this descriptive process is that it is simple yet extremely powerful. Consider the following two responses to the question "Where do you live?"

Response 1: "I live at 1234 Snowflake Court."

Response 2: "You go down this street for two blocks, turn right, and go down three houses to the one with the blue door and the oak tree in front."

The first response, an address measured against a fixed reference, assumes familiarity with the streets in an area perhaps as large as a city. To make use of that answer, you also have to know where Snowflake Court is relative to your present location. Although the address might be complete, it is only valuable to you if you are familiar with the city. The second response describes the procedure by which you would get to the house, given your present position and orientation. It is a purely "local" description in that it makes no assumption that you know any of the streets in the community. It assumes only that you can follow simple instructions that make incremental changes in your present position. If you were in a strange city, you probably would find the second answer much more useful than the first. Each instruction is given with respect to the position and orientation of the participant at the end of the previous instruction. This descriptive procedure is identical to that used in turtle graphics.

Just as descriptive procedures make sense, the exceptional power of turtle graphics makes it most valuable for illustrating important properties of geometric figures (for example, curvature). Its similarity to natural descriptive language has made turtle graphics a most powerful vehicle in allowing people to discover important geometric principles on their own.

My first exposure to turtle graphics came when I worked at the Xerox Palo Alto Research Center—the home of the language Smalltalk. Although Smalltalk supports an exceptional turtle graphics environment, it was implemented on computer systems that were far too expensive for the average consumer. I have used several turtle environments over the years, including computer languages such as WSFN (Which Stands For Nothing) and "toys" such as Milton Bradley's Big Trak. The simplicity and exceptional power of Lynx allows the user to concentrate on the application of the language rather than on the language's structure. As a result, the reader will find the computer to be a comfortable tool of discovery—not a time-consuming object of study.

My experience has shown that, whatever the form—an actual robot or a graphic display—turtle environments are liked especially by people who previously have been afraid to learn how to program a computer. If you have never worked with a computer before (and you have access to a computer that uses Lynx), you will find this book to be a most gentle guide to a very powerful tool.

I have been encouraged to write books in this area by many members of the research, product design, and development community who are actively generating user-friendly languages. Over the years I've written many books on the topic, and it is time to update these books to reach a new audience of enthusiasts.

It is a pleasure to acknowledge my debt to those who have labored long and hard to develop user friendly computer languages. I am also indebted to my friends in the educational computer community—particularly Gary Stager and Peter Skillen—for their willingness to provide me with a kind ear, spirited discussions, and an occasional forum for the expression of my desire to improve education.

Most of all, I am indebted to the children and artists with whom I have shared my efforts in this area over the past few decades. Were it not for the joyful inquisitiveness of these people, this book would not exist.

David Thornburg

Lake Barrington. IL, March 2021

1 - What This Book Is All About

If I knew what two and two were I would say Four!
Saying of the Mulla Nasrudin, from *The Subtleties of the Inimitable Mulla Nasrudin*, Idries Shah

This is a book about discovery—the discoveries each of us can make when finding beauty in geometric patterns, beauty in mathematics, and beauty in computer programming.

It is easy to see how one might find beauty in geometric patterns; this beauty forms the foundation of nature and art. We are continually entranced by geometric form—the symmetry of a butterfly's wings, the spiral of a snail's shell, the facets of a crystal—and each of these natural occurrences is perceived as having beauty associated with it. The hands of people have produced geometric art since marks were first made on cave walls or stones were first fashioned into tools. From the Pyramids and the Parthenon to the finest gold-link chain, the beauty of geometric form is clearly present for all who care to find it.

Underlying the geometric pattern that we experience with our eyes lies a more subtle pattern of mathematical beauty, which is experienced intellectually—a collection of unifying principles that govern the arrangement and shapes of objects, both natural and crafted. To glimpse this power of mathematics, consider four regular geometric figures—a triangle, a square, a pentagon, and a hexagon.

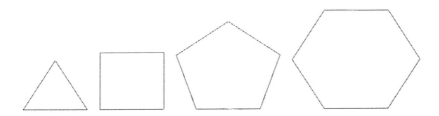

Each of these simple polygons has sides of equal length. Suppose you wanted to make a tile floor using polygons of only one type. You can tile a floor with triangles.

You can tile a floor with squares.

And you can tile a floor with hexagons.

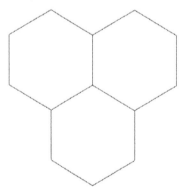

However, no matter how hard you try, you cannot tile a floor with regular pentagons.

Why is this? The answer to this question is found in a beautiful mathematical discovery of a unifying property that applies to all shapes that can be drawn on a flat surface. This concept (and many more) will be explored in this book.

Along with the beauty of form and mathematics, there is another beauty we will explore—the beauty of descriptive procedures that use mathematical concepts to create pictures of our geometric forms on a computer display screen. Through these descriptive procedures we can command the computer to generate an unlimited array of pictures, many of which we might find nearly impossible to create with any other medium.

You might wonder how an electrical device as complex and technical as a computer can be an effective tool for creative expression. Many people who have avoided using computers have done so for a variety of reasons. Some feel that you have to be "good at math" to use a computer. Some feel that a computer is useful only for balancing checkbooks or for performing other tasks that are clearly defined in advance. Some feel that the computer is so hard to use that by the time you have learned how, you have forgotten what you wanted to do with it in the first place.

These ideas can be dispelled as myths. Whatever the computer has been before, it is now also something else. The computer today can be a tool for discovery and creative expression. It can be as malleable as a piece of clay and as powerful as the very ideas it helps to express.

To get full benefit from this book, you should have access to a computer system with a Web browser like Chrome so you can use the language Lynx. In the remainder of this chapter we will trace the events that brought the power of this programming environment into people's homes.

Computers for People

Fifty years ago, computers were very hard to use. First you had to spend a lot of time learning to write computer programs in a language that was specialized for your application. If you were a scientist or engineer, you might use a computer language called FORTRAN (FORmula TRANslation). If your application was business related, you might use COBOL (COmmon Business Oriented Language). Once you learned the language, you would then generate the program statements for the problem you wanted to solve. Next, you would have to punch these commands onto special cards, which you then carried to a computer center. Here you would pass your stack of cards to a highly trained computer operator, who would place your task in line with hundreds of other jobs being performed by a massive central computer. If you were lucky, you could pick up the results of your program an hour or so later. The massive computer probably spent less than a few seconds performing the tasks you requested; the time delay was caused by one central computer serving the needs of many users.

This mode of computer usage is not very inviting to those who would like to experiment with programming. In fact, the only people who used computers 50 years ago were those who were highly motivated to do so. Whatever computing was then, it certainly was not casual.

Attempts to make the central computer more responsive to the needs of its users resulted in the creation of "time-sharing" systems. In the time-sharing environment a central computer was connected by telephone lines to computer terminals located in each user's office. For the first time, this allowed interaction between the user and the computer while the computer was working on the user's task. Although time sharing greatly increased people's access to computers: it was a pale compromise when compared to the revolution that happened next.

The most important year in the development of computers was 1977. It was then that affordable small computer systems were first being sold to people who had had no previous experience with them, with the Commodore PET, the Apple II, and the Radio Shack TRS-80 leading the pack.

The development of the personal computer promised to have an impact as great as that of the automobile. Millions of these small computers are being used for everything from games to business, education, and communication. There seems to be no limit to the application of the personal computer; and yet, until quite recently, the revolution was incomplete.

For the computer to be truly useful, it needed to be easily programmable by its user. Furthermore, although the programming language had to be easy to use, it also needed to have sufficient power to allow it continued use as the user became more proficient. It was the development of powerful user-friendly computer languages that formed the basis for the second revolution.

Languages for people to use with computers

The function of language is to aid communication. Communication implies the interchange of ideas or expressions between two or more parties. If I talk to you in English, you probably will understand what I say. If you talk to me in Swahili, I will not understand you, because Swahili is not a language I speak. In order to be useful for communication, a language has to be shared by all parties.

How do we pick languages for computers? At one extreme, we could send the computer the patterns of ones and zeroes that form the elements of its computational framework. Although this language of the machine may make it work effectively, it is so different from natural languages that it is a poor choice. On the other extreme, we might choose a language such as English. Although this would seem to simplify our task, English is too imprecise to serve effectively as a computer language. Consider, for example, the phrase pretty little girl's school. Does this refer to a school for pretty little girls, to a pretty school for little girls, or to something else altogether?

It is far better to devise computer languages that form intermediate compromises between these extremes. The interactive computer language BASIC (Beginner's All-purpose Symbolic Instruction Code) was the principal programming environment for the first few years of the personal computer revolution. BASIC was well suited for this task because it used English language "keywords" to instruct the computer to perform well-defined tasks. By using words in carefully defined, non ambiguous ways, it became possible for the user to generate his or her own programs. But certain characteristics of BASIC showed its flaws.

Like natural languages, computer languages have rules of grammar and vocabularies. The rules of grammar are fairly rigidly fixed for most languages, but BASIC also has a fixed vocabulary. The restriction implied by a fixed vocabulary was quite severe. Imagine how effective English would be if, for example, no new words had entered the language since the time of Shakespeare. What would we call computers, televisions, or automobiles?

For natural languages to survive, they must be extensible; new words must be able to enter the language as they are needed. The vitality this extensibility gives to natural languages also applies to computer languages. For example, because BASIC programmers were forced to live with a fixed vocabulary, the skilled BASIC programmer found that the language becomes quite cumbersome for the expression of sophisticated programming ideas.

Research on extensible computer languages has been conducted in university and industrial research centers for many years. Central to these new languages is the idea that the user should be able to use carefully defined primitive instructions to build new commands into the language and then give those new functions their own names. Lynx is a language of this type.

Lynx is easily one of the most powerful and user-friendly computer languages ever implemented on a personal computer. It has an extraordinarily powerful graphics environment (whose characteristics will be amply illustrated in this book); it can be used with very little formal instruction; and it can be extended by the user as desired.

The power of Lynx must be experienced to be believed. Many people who are familiar with other languages embrace Lynx as being among the best computer languages they have seen. As you work with Lynx yourself, you may see why the enthusiasm for this language is so great.

2 – Lynx and the Turtle: A Gentle Guide to a Powerful Language

"When we were little ... we went to school in the sea. The master was an old Turtle-we used to call him Tortoise." "Why did you call him Tortoise if he wasn't one?" Alice asked. "We called him Tortoise because he taught us," said the Mock Turtle angrily. "Really, you are very dense."
Alice's Adventures in Wonderland

To get full benefit from this book, you will need to have access to a computer system that uses the language Lynx. That covers almost every computer, Chromebook or tablet available today. If you have a browser like Chrome, you're all set.

Although color lets you add another dimension to your pictures, it isn't necessary for anything we will do.

Your projects will all be saved in the "cloud." This means they can be accessed from any computer you're using. But it also means you have to remember to save your work regularly! I can't stress this enough.

The rest of this chapter is devoted to the basic mechanics of getting Lynx started on the computer and to the basic characteristics and commands of the graphics system. If you are already familiar with these topics, you may skip to the next chapter if you wish.

Getting Started with Lynx

Launch Lynx at lynxcoding.club and log in. Next, click on the **CREATE** button.

Once you do this, you'll see an image with three panes. Yours will all be blank except for a small black turtle sitting in the middle of the graphics pane on the right side. There are two text panes. The one on the left is where you'll add procedures of your own, and the one beneath the graphics pane is the command pane where you'll enter commands and see any text messages being sent by your programs.

The objects you see on display are just a sample of the kinds of things you might see when creating your own programs.

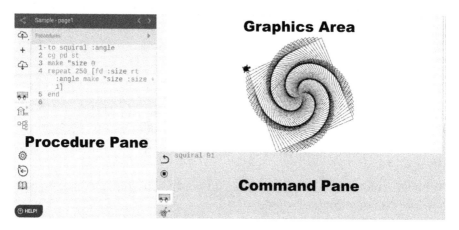

For now, try typing something in the command pane like

HELLO

and notice how the cursor moves along as you type. You are creating a message to send to your computer. To send this message, press the **RETURN** key. As soon as you do this, the computer will display this message:

I DON'T KNOW HOW TO HELLO

and present you with a fresh flashing cursor.

Well, the computer doesn't appear to understand our greeting because HELLO is neither a primitive, nor a procedure we've defined; but we did learn something very important. To send commands to the computer, you must press the **RETURN** key after you have typed the instructions you want the computer to follow. Later you may find that you will type instructions that are more than one line long. In this case you will keep on typing until you are done and then press the **RETURN** key at the very end, rather than at the end of each line of text on the screen.

Everything you type for a while will be typed in the Command pane. We'll get to the Procedures pane later in this book.

Introducing the Turtle

The turtle is a powerful Lynx object that lets us draw pictures on the graphics work area. If you don't see your turtle at the center of the graphics screen, click the "+" button between the two cloud images on the left side of the screen.

It is convenient to think of the turtle as a robot to which we send commands. The two most important types of commands at our disposal are those that make the turtle move in a straight line and those that make the turtle turn. By using combinations of these commands, we can instruct the turtle to draw almost anything we wish on the display. The pictures are drawn by a "pen" that is carried by the turtle. We can change the pen color, lift it up, set it down, and change the pen to an eraser. Later on, you'll learn how to change the shape of the turtle. When the turtle first starts out, it is holding a black pen that is "up" (not ready to draw). In the Command pane, type

```
PENDOWN
FORWARD 100
```

As soon as you press **RETURN**, the turtle will draw a line from its starting (home) position to a point 100 units away.

It is important to start with the PENDOWN command the first time you give commands in the Command pane. This is because Lynx starts with the pen up, so it will not draw a line.

Next, try entering the command

```
LEFT 90
```

The turtle orientation turns 90 degrees to the left. Now enter

FORWARD 500

the turtle will move off the screen and reappear from the right side (a feature called "wrapping").

To bring the turtle into its home position once again, enter

CLEARGRAPHICS or CG

Now before continuing, I want to touch on a few things. First, I'll be writing instructions in all uppercase, even though Lynx doesn't care what case you use. Second, there are lots of popular commands that have two-letter equivalents. See if you can tell what these commands do:

FD
BK
LT
RT
CG
PD
PU

As soon as you start typing a command, a pop-up screen will show you the two-letter versions along with the fully spelled words.

Next, let's learn how to make the turtle do some more things with the pen, such as pick it up, change its color, and so on. Recall that when the turtle first starts out, it is holding a pen in the up (non-drawing) position. To see how to move this pen up and down, try the following. Enter the following commands

CLEARGRAPHICS
PENDOWN
FORWARD 50
PENUP
RIGHT 90
FORWARD 50

```
PENDOWN
FORWARD 50
```

As you can see from this figure, there is a 50-unit gap in the line as it turns the corner. Now that we have seen what **PENUP** and **PENDOWN** do, let's see how to get the turtle to erase a line once it has drawn it. Enter

```
CLEARGRAPHICS
FORWARD 100
```

to draw a line on the screen. Now, to erase it, enter

```
PENERASE BACK 100
```

and, presto, the original line is erased. To draw a line again, just enter

```
PENDOWN FORWARD 100
```

So far, we have worked with a black pen against a white background. Lynx lets us change pen and background colors independently.

To set the pen to a new color, just enter the command

SETCOLOUR X or **SETC X** where X is a number. There are hundreds of colors from which you can choose. To make life a bit easier, you can use a color's name, for example.,

```
SETC 'BLACK'
```

Notice that the color name is bracketed in single quotes. This should be applied to variable names (but not their contents) and maybe take a little getting used to if you are migrating from an older version of Logo. Also, fior my US readers, note the spelling of **SETCOLOUR**. The reason for the "U" is that Lynx was created in Canada which uses different spellings from the US version of English for some words. However, if you live in the US, you'll be pleased to know that **SETCOLOR** works just as well!

SETBG is the command that changes the background color. It uses the same color table as **SETPC**. Before concluding this chapter, we have a magic trick for the turtle to perform. Ready? Enter

```
CLEARGRAPHICS or CG
```

You can see the turtle in the middle of the screen. Next, enter

HT

and, poof, the turtle becomes hidden from view. You can convince yourself that the turtle is still there by having it draw some lines. To see the turtle again, enter

ST

You may want to keep the turtle visible while you are learning how to use the turtle graphics. Once you are comfortable with this graphics environment, you will probably want to make the turtle invisible at the end so that it doesn't interfere with your drawing.

Because of our emphasis on graphics, you may be thinking that Lynx is primarily a graphics language. Nothing could be further from the truth. As we progress through this book, other aspects of Lynx will be presented as well.

We packed a tremendous amount of information into this chapter, so you might want to experiment some more with these commands and instructions before going on. Above all, don't feel that you have to commit this chapter to memory before proceeding. The best way to learn Lynx is to use it.

> *Note: You can do the projects in this book using the free 30-day trial version of Lynx at* lynxcoding.club. *After that, you can upgrade to the full version for just a few dollars. For classes and clubs, you can purchase a low-cost school or club site license that allows a teacher to coordinate groups of student accounts.*
>
> *All the features we'll use in this book are available in all versions.*

3 – Lines and Figures: The Turtle Moves On

Beauty is the harmony and concord of all parts, achieved in such a manner that nothing could be taken away or altered except for the worse. Leon Battista Alberti (1404–1472)

Each of these four figures here has something in common with the others.

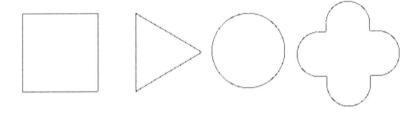

They are all closed figures. This means that each has a boundary that separates its inside from its outside. The first two figures (the square and the triangle) are examples of regular polygons. The third figure is a circle, and the last is a meandering curve that produces a closed figure.

It is common to think of such patterns in a static way—a way that describes their existence as completed objects. In reality, however, any figure or form is created by a process—a sequence of events that moves from the universe without the expression of the figure to the universe with the figure in it. Since nothing in nature can happen instantaneously, anything that exists does so by virtue of the process that created it. When we see only the finished form, we often lose the information used in its creation. This information is often as interesting as the final form itself. What is less obvious is that a description of the process by which an object is created can be a more succinct and understandable representation of the object than a description based on the final form alone. As we embark on our exploration of the generative processes for various forms, you will have ample opportunity to test this hypothesis for yourself.

A Closed Path

If we start with the turtle in the center of the screen (by typing CG, for example), we can generate a picture of a square by having the turtle draw a continuous line as it moves in a square path.

```
FORWARD 80
RIGHT 90
FORWARD 80
RIGHT 90
FORWARD 80
RIGHT 90
FORWARD 80
RIGHT 90
```

The process that is described by this statement conveys the essence of a square, since a square has four equal sides and four equal angles (of 90 degrees each). This process provides us with a purely local description of a square. The same procedure will generate a square from any starting location and orientation of the turtle. To see this, we can use the Lynx command SETPOS to set the position of the turtle to other screen locations from which we can draw squares. The SETPOS command needs information in the form of a list of horizontal (x) and vertical (y) coordinates for the turtle. For example, enter

```
CG REPEAT 4 [FORWARD 100 RIGHT 90]
```

to see a square drawn from the turtle's home position. You can see that the command REPEAT executes the instructions FORWARD 100 and RIGHT 90 four times. This saves a lot of typing!

Next, enter

```
PU SETPOS [-60 -20] PD
```

to move the turtle to a new location.

Then use the same command sequence for the square:

```
REPEAT 4 [FORWARD 100 RIGHT 90]
```

Now let's change the pen color to orange, rotate the turtle by 30 degrees, and draw the square again:

```
SETC 'ORANGE'  RIGHT 30 REPEAT 4 [FORWARD 100 RIGHT 90]
```

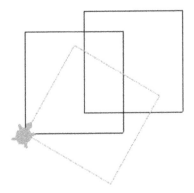

This example illustrates the fact that the command

```
REPEAT 4 [FORWARD 100 RIGHT 90]
```

describes a 100-unit square at any turtle location or orientation. The beauty of the process descriptions we will use is that they describe the properties of the objects we are creating independently from the locations of these objects in space.

Before discovering some other properties of procedures that generate closed figures, we will digress to a topic that is relevant to all geometric forms—symmetry.

Symmetry

Patterns—whether natural or handmade—often have a repetitive underlying structure that we call symmetry. These three figures will help to illustrate different ways that figures can be symmetrical.

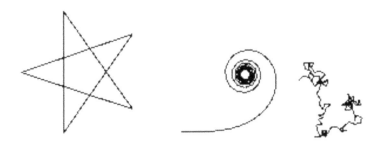

If you were to group these figures on the basis of what they have in common, you would probably group the star with the spiral and exclude the random scribble shown in the last figure. The star and the spiral are similar in that they were both generated by a completely determined rule that could be deduced by studying the finished figures. The random scribble wasn't the result of any such rule.

Both the star and the spiral are symmetrical figures, although each has a different kind of symmetry. Looking at the star, we can see that it was made by repeating a subunit five times. This subunit draws a line and turns by some angle. Because each of these subunits was the same—both in the length of the line and in the turning angle—the resulting figure has a rotational symmetry. If you were to make a star of the same size and lay it over the one in the figure, you would find five rotational positions at which the two stars would overlap perfectly. The star has fivefold rotational symmetry. Using the same process, you can convince yourself that a square has fourfold rotational symmetry and that a rectangle has twofold rotational symmetry.

Star Figures

Complete figures, such as a star, have a very important property. As the star was being made, it went from a point of incompletion to the point at which it was finished. At most stages of its development it was not a star; then, at the end, it finally became a star.

Prior to the last step, we did not have a figure that had the symmetry or form of the final result. Only when the last step was taken was the star finished. At this point no additional lines could be added without changing the nature of the figure.

We will refer to figures of this type as figures displaying static symmetry. Static symmetry is found in snowflakes, mineral crystals, floor tiles, wallpaper patterns, and myriad other objects that we can call complete or finished.

The spiral is an example of a figure displaying a different kind of symmetry. The spiral is sufficiently well organized that we can deduce the procedure for its creation by studying the spiral itself. Even without knowing this procedure explicitly, you probably could continue to extend it yourself, based on the portion already present.

The symmetry displayed by the spiral is one of proportion. Each segment of the spiral arm is proportionately related to the preceding section. The spiral is always ready to grow; there is never a point at which it becomes complete.

One consequence of this is that the spiral has a property called handedness. Our spiral grows by turning to the left, and thus is called a left-handed spiral.

We can just as easily create a right-handed spiral.

Because figures of this type are never finished, we will call them figures of dynamic symmetry. Dynamic symmetry is found in sea shells, flowers, pinecones, whirlpools, woven baskets, and in many other objects that can be enlarged proportionately by repeating the same process that created the object in the first place. As we progress through this book, we will explore many examples of both static and dynamic symmetry.

4 – Paths and Procedures

And then there was Rose. Rose was her name and would she have been Rose if her name had not been Rose. She used to think and then she used to think again. Would she have been Rose if her name had not been Rose and would she have been Rose if she had been a twin.
– Gertrude Stein, *The World is Round*

As we mentioned in Chapter 1, the power of natural languages derives from their ability to be extended. Imagine how useless English would be if no new words were introduced to the language since the time of Shakespeare. What would we call televisions, telephones, automobiles, or computers? Natural languages are extended as a result of people's needs to express thoughts whose expression is too cumbersome for the existing vocabulary.

A computer language that is extensible has two features. First, the user benefits from being able to replace complex definitions by a single word, which ther becomes part of the computer's lexicon. Second, extensibility allows the language designer to focus on the primitive commands from which new words can be defined. By not focusing on the wealth of applications for which the language may be applied, the primitive commands can be combined into new procedures by each user, who in effect creates a personal version of the language, tailored to his or her specific needs and interests.

Simple Procedures

All the commands we have used thus far are Lynx primitives. The creation of extensions to Lynx occurs through the definition of procedures. Suppose, for example, that we wanted to have the turtle draw a 50-unit square in response to the word SQUARE. If you enter this word now, you will probably see the following message:

I DON'T KNOW HOW TO SQUARE

This message lets you know that SQUARE is not a word in Lynx's built-in library of procedures. To change this, enter the following in the Procedures pane:

```
TO SQUARE
REPEAT 4 [FORWARD 100 RIGHT 90]
END
```

All Lynx procedures start with the word TO and must finish with the command END. The numbers at the beginning of each line are there to help you find any errors if your procedure doesn't work. These are added automatically as you are typing.

```
Procedures
  1  TO SQUARE
  2  REPEAT 4 [FORWARD 100 RIGHT 90]
  3  END
```

To see if Lynx now "knows" about the word SQUARE, click your mouse in the Command pane and enter

CG SQUARE

When you press RETURN after entering SQUARE, a 100-unit square appears on the screen.

Thus the Lynx language has just been extended to include the procedure SQUARE.

This procedure can now be treated just as if it were a primitive command. For example, try to anticipate what this command will do:

```
CG REPEAT 6 [SQUARE RIGHT 60]
```

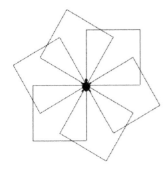

Now that you know how to extend Lynx, you should know how to save your extensions so that you won't have to re-create them each time you use the computer. To save all of your procedures, create a name for your project in the upper left black box (I called mine **My first procedure**). And click on the cloud image with the picture of an arrow pointing up.

Your files will be saved online so you can access them from any computer you have access to. Since you will end up with quite a few files in the cloud, it is a good idea to pick file names that give a clue as to their contents. To avoid confusion, it is also a good idea to use a filename that is not the same as the name of any procedure in the file.

Finally, and this is *very* important, save your projects often—the computer will not do it for you! If you don't, everything you created since you started working will be lost when you shut down Lynx.

To see the names of the procedures saved on your account, just click on the cloud with the arrow pointing down, and choose **My Projects**

and the screen will display the names of the files as well as provide the ability to load them to your workspace.

Procedures of One Variable

We have a procedure that draws a 100-unit square, but suppose that you want to define a procedure that lets you draw a square of any size. In our previous procedure we had the turtle move forward by a fixed number of units each time. To make a procedure that draws a square of any size, we need to find a way to have the turtle move forward by some number of units that won't be specified until we use the procedure. Instead of using FORWARD 100, we need to replace the 100 with a variable that is specified when SQUARE is used.

In Lynx, words can be used as names under which information is stored. This means, for example, that we can use a word such as SIZE to contain the number of steps we want for each side of the SQUARE. SIZE is the name of the variable, and the thing that SIZE contains would be the length of each side.

Since variables are a very important part of Lynx, we will spend a little more time discussing them before building our new SQUARE procedure. Lynx variables can contain any of three types of information: numbers, words, and lists. To see how variables work, let's do an experiment. To make a Lynx variable contain something, we use the MAKE command. We can make the variable TEST contain the number 4 by entering MAKE 'TEST' 4. Note that the quotation mark is straight, not curly. Curly marks won't work, although you'd only see them if you pasted some text from a document that uses them.

To show text on the screen, click on the **+ symbol** on the left side of the screen. From the pop-up menu choose Text. This will put a small text box on the graphics screen.

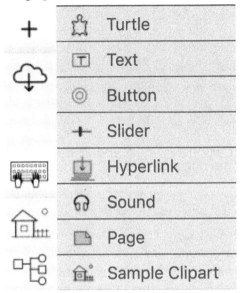

When you click inside the text box, you'll see ways to change the font, text size, box size, and other things.

Later on we'll show how to rename this box and do other cool things. For now, just set the type size to Large and drag the lower right corner of the box to make it a bit bigger. Click outside the box to close the top menu.

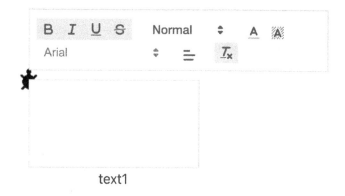

text1

To see that the word TEST contains the number 4, we can print the thing contained in TEST on the screen by entering

PRINT THING 'TEST'

The number 4 appears in the upper left corner of the text box as soon as you press **RETURN**.

Using MAKE and PRINT in this way, you will see that a Lynx variable can hold words and lists as well as numbers. (Remember that words need a single quotation mark at the beginning and end, and that lists are enclosed in square brackets.)

It is quite common to want to use the thing associated with a variable, and typing THING each time can be cumbersome. To make life easier, Lynx has a short form for THING. To see how it works, enter the following:

MAKE 'TEST' 64 PRINT :TEST

The number 64 will appear on the screen, showing that the short form :TEST is equivalent to THING 'TEST'.

By the way, if you want you can print to the Command pane without having to make a Text box. Just use SHOW instead of PRINT, e.g.,

MAKE 'TEST' 64 SHOW :TEST

Personally, I like this method better since it avoids cluttering the graphics screen.

We are now ready to build our new SQUARE procedure. We will use the word SIZE to denote the length of our square's side. To define the new procedure, first erase any old copy that might be in the workspace.Next, enter

```
TO SQUARE :SIZE
REPEAT 4 [FORWARD :SIZE RIGHT 90]
END
```

Notice that the thing associated with SIZE appears in two places—in the first line and after the word FORWARD. Now enter:

```
SQUARE 20
SQUARE 40
SQUARE 80
```

In the Command pane to see three squares drawn on the screen.

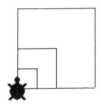

Notice that each number you entered is passed by the SQUARE procedure to the FORWARD command inside this procedure. The SQUARE procedure can thus be used to create a square of any size.

Polygons and Pathways

The square is but one example of a regular polygon. One can construct regular polygons with any number of sides greater than two. Let's examine some of the simpler polygons. Enter

```
CG REPEAT 3 [FORWARD 50 RIGHT 120]
```

This puts a triangle on the screen. Next, let's create a square by entering

```
REPEAT 4 [FORWARD 50 RIGHT 90]
```

To see a regular pentagon, enter

```
REPEAT 5 [FORWARD 50 RIGHT 72]
```

and to draw a hexagon, enter REPEAT 6 [FORWARD 50 RIGHT 60]

What do these four figures have in common? They are all closed paths, since the turtle always ends up exactly where it starts. They also were drawn with identical side lengths. In addition to all this, however, there is something these figures share with all simple closed paths—something that will let us create a procedure to draw any regular polygon we wish.

The Turtle's Total Trip

If you study the commands that created each polygon you will notice that as the number of sides increases, the amount the turtle turns at each corner decreases. To draw a triangle, we turn by 120 degrees; a square results from a turn of 90 degrees; and a pentagon and hexagon use turning angles of 72 and 60 degrees, respectively.

The discovery we can make comes from looking at the total amount turned for each polygon. The following table shows the results of this calculation.

Amount Turned At Each Corner	Number Of Turns	Total Amount Turned	Polygon
120	3	360	Triangle
90	4	360	Square
72	5	360	Pentagon
60	6	360	Hexagon

From this table, we see that the total amount turned in following any simple polygonal path is 360 degrees.

You can test this rule for any simple closed figure (one that does not cross over itself). In adding up the angles, you must subtract turns to the left from turns to the right, since if you turn to the right by some amount and then turn to the left by the same amount, your turns cancel each other out. Consider this hexagon. It was drawn by the following commands:

```
FORWARD 50
RIGHT 120
FORWARD 60
LEFT 60
FORWARD 60
RIGHT 120
FORWARD 50
RIGHT 60
FORWARD 60
RIGHT 60
FORWARD 60
RIGHT 60
```

If we add up all the turns to the right we get 420 degrees; if we then subtract the 60-degree turn to the left, we see that the net turning angle is 420 – 60, or 360 degrees.

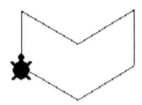

The name of the rule we have found is the **Total Turtle Trip Theorem**. Using this rule, we can define a new procedure that draws any regular polygon. If we specify the number of sides in the polygon, then the amount turned at each corner is 360 divided by the number of sides. Lynx uses the solidus (/) to indicate division. The general polygon procedure is as follows:

```
TO POLY :SIZE :SIDES
REPEAT :SIDES [FORWARD :SIZE RIGHT 360 / :SIDES]
END
```

Let's try out this procedure for all polygons from triangles to nonagons (nine sides). Enter

```
CG
POLY 40 3
POLY 40 4
POLY 40 5
POLY 40 6
POLY 40 7
POLY 40 8
POLY 40 9
```

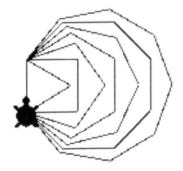

As you can see, the POLY procedure works perfectly.

The total trip theorem is one of the most significant rules you will learn in this book. We will be exploring its ramifications in the chapters that follow.

5 – Tiles and Tessellations

Of all the constraints on nature, the most far-reaching are imposed by space. For space itself has a structure that influences the shape of every existing thing. – Peter Stevens, *Patterns in Nature*

We are surrounded by patterns that fill two-dimensional space. Some of these patterns, such as murals and stained-glass windows, are finished works of art that are whole in themselves and are not designed to be replicated as repeated patterns. Other figures, such as those found on wallpaper, for example, consist of a basic motif that is designed to be repeated as many times as is necessary to cover a surface.

The design of motifs that can be replicated to fill two-dimensional space is an interesting topic for study. The basic motif is chosen for its visually attractive elements; when it is repeated in both horizontal and vertical directions, it should create an overall pattern that is also visually pleasing.

Compared to other replicating patterns, wallpaper designs are fairly unconstrained. One can start with almost any simple figure and repeat it at points on a regular grid to form an overall pattern. To see how a wallpaper design might be made, let's choose a simple motif-a five-pointed star (stars are sufficiently interesting that we will study them in detail in the next chapter).

```
TO MOTIF
REPEAT 5 [FORWARD 20 RIGHT 144]
END
```

If you now enter

```
MOTIF
```

you will see the basic pattern.

Next, let's create the procedures that allow us to replicate this pattern in a wallpaper design. To do this, we must move the turtle to the upper left edge of the screen. Then we need a procedure that uses the procedure MOTIF, turns the turtle to the right, moves it by some amount (the repeat distance), and turns the turtle back to its original position. If we keep using this procedure, we should get a horizontal chain of stars on the screen. See if you can create this procedure yourself. Here is one way to do it:

```
TO HORPATTERN :STEP
MOTIF
PENUP
RIGHT 90
FORWARD :STEP
LEFT 90
PENDOWN
END
```

We will pick the position [-400 200] as the starting point and draw a line of stars. Enter

```
CG
PENUP
SETPOS [-130 75]
PENDOWN
REPEAT 10 [HORPATTERN 50]
```

As you can see, we now have a row of stars. To turn this into a wallpaper pattern, we need to have a procedure that moves the turtle back to the horizontal starting position and then moves it down the screen by some distance. The procedure VERTSTEP should do this:

```
TO VERTSTEP :STEP
PENUP
SETX -130
RIGHT 180
FORWARD :STEP
LEFT 180
PENDOWN
END
```

(NOTE: The command SETX moves the turtle to the horizontal (x) position specified without changing the vertical (y) position at all. As you might imagine, there is also a corresponding command, SETY.)

To see how our new procedure works, enter

```
VERTSTEP 50
REPEAT 10 [HORPATTERN 50]
```

to get a new row of stars.

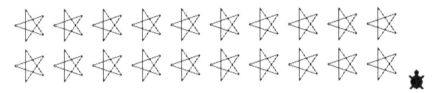

Finally, we can create a "wallpaper generator" to fill the screen with an array of figures generated by MOTIF:

```
TO PAPER :XSTEP :YSTEP
PENUP
SETPOS [-130 75]
PENDOWN
REPEAT 5 [REPEAT 10 [HORPATTERN :XSTEP] VERTSTEP
:YSTEP]
END
```

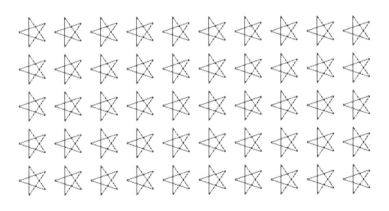

[NOTE: When entering long lines (such as the fifth line of the foregoing procedure) do not press **RETURN** until you have finished the entire entry (for example, until after you have typed :YSTEP]). Lynx will automatically break the line at the edge of the screen as many times as are necessary until you complete the entry.]

To get the full benefit of PAPER, examine the pattern you get with PAPER 40 50. Try other values to see what you get.

In this pattern (PAPER 40 50), the stars just touch each other to form a closed network pattern.

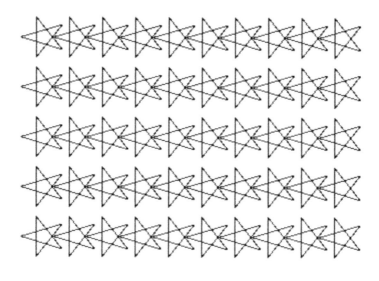

Space-Filling Patterns

We will study patterns that are more reminiscent of tile floors. Patterns made from such perfectly interlocking motifs are called tessellations.

How many tessellating patterns are there? There is a limitless number of patterns that tessellate, just as there is a limitless number of patterns that don't tessellate. We will discover a rule that lets us find out in advance whether certain motifs can be used to tessellate a plane.

Let's start with regular polygons. In Chapter 1, we mentioned that one could fill a plane with triangles,squares, and hexagons, but not with pentagons. Starting with equilateral triangles, we can see that there are any number of ways that identical triangles can be arranged to fill space. These figures show two examples.

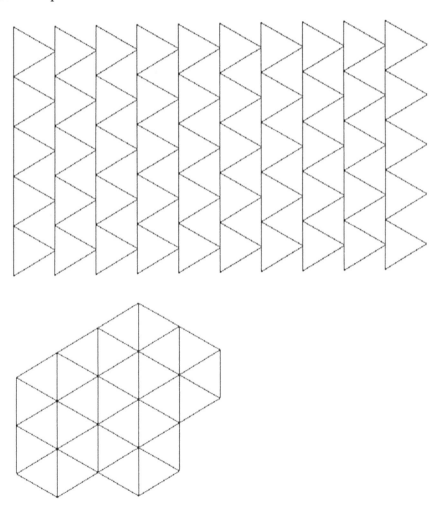

The same is true of squares.

Hexagons, however, are unique. There is only one way to arrange hexagons so that they fill space.

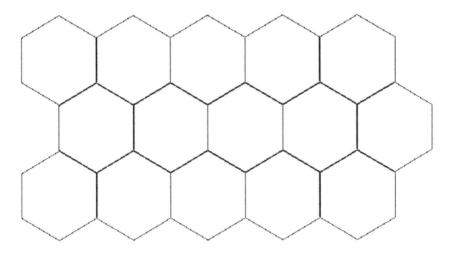

The hexagon lies at the boundary dividing regular polygons that can tessellate (those with three, four, or six sides) from those that, by themselves, cannot fill a plane (those with any number of sides more than six). But what about the five-sided pentagon? We saw in the first chapter that it couldn't be used to tile a plane. We will show why soon.

What happens if we try to tessellate a plane with a polygon that has more than six sides? Let's try using an octagon and see what we get. To generate an octagon, we can use the POLY procedure defined in a previous chapter. If this procedure is not presently in your Lynx workspace, you should retrieve it from the computer or create a new copy. Next, we need to modify MOTIF to draw an octagon. First edit the procedure:

```
TO MOTIF
POLY 20 8
END
```

If you enter

`CG MOTIF`

you will see an octagon on the screen.

To see an attempt to tessellate a plane with octagons, enter

`CG PAPER 48 48`

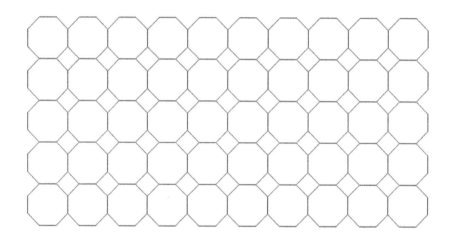

The resulting pattern shows that space can be filled with an interlocking arrangement of octagons and squares. Although polygons with more than six sides can't fill space by themselves, they can be part of a space-filling pattern that uses other polygons.

To see a major property of all tessellating figures, let's start by looking at a node where three hexagons join. The turtle is at the point of interest.

Suppose that we place the turtle at some location away from this point and face it to the right.

If we were to draw any closed figure around the node from this starting point, the turtle would have to turn by 360 degrees. We know this result from the Total Turtle Trip Theorem. Suppose that we move along an arc in the first hexagon. (The interior angle of a hexagon is 120 degrees.)

If we repeat this movement for the second and third hexagons, we turn an additional 240 degrees, giving us 360 degrees overall.

From this example, we can see that, for polygons to tessellate, the sum of the interior angles measured around each node where three or more polygons meet must be 360 degrees.

Notice that the angle of concern is different from the one by which the turtle turns when it draws the polygon in the first place. To draw an angle for an equilateral triangle, for example, the turtle turns by 120 degrees.

The interior angle is the amount by which the turtle would then have to turn to be pointing back along the original direction. In our example this is 60 degrees.

The sum of the interior and exterior angles is always 180 degrees for any angle. Using this information, we can determine which polygons tessellate and which do not. For equilateral triangles, the interior angle is 60 degrees. If we divide this into 360 degrees, we see that exactly six such triangles can meet at a node and exactly fill a two-dimensional space. Thus, as we already know, we can make a tessellating pattern from triangles.

For squares, the interior angle is 90 degrees. Four squares meet at a corner to give exactly 360 degrees. For hexagons, the interior angle is 120 degrees, thus allowing exactly three hexagons to meet at a corner.

But what about the pentagon? To draw a regular pentagon, the turtle must turn by 72 degrees at each corner. This yields an interior angle of 180 – 72, or 108 degrees. If we place three pentagons together, the total combined angle is 324 degrees—not enough to fill space. Yet four pentagons give 432 degrees—far too much. This is why it is impossible to tessellate a plane with regular pentagonal tiles.

We can use the same rules when analyzing tessellations that use combinations of polygons, such as the combination of octagons and squares. In that case, the octagons have interior angles of 180 – 45, or 135 degrees. Two octagons meet to give a combined angle of 270 degrees. The 90-degree corner of a square brings us exactly to the desired value of 360 degrees, thus confirming what we already knew from experiment.

Thus the total trip theorem has led us to another valuable rule—one that governs all tessellating figures.

You should experiment with mixtures of regular polygons to find other combinations that produce tessellations. For example, you might want to analyze the different types of nodes in the tessellating figure shown here.

Other Space-Filling Figures

Tessellating figures are in no way limited to regular polygons. The chevron-shaped figure we drew in the previous chapter tessellates quite nicely. To see this, erase MOTIF and replace it with the procedure

```
TO MOTIF
FORWARD 50
RIGHT 120
FORWARD 60
LEFT 60
FORWARD 60
RIGHT 120
FORWARD 50
RIGHT 60
FORWARD 60
RIGHT 60
FORWARD 60
RIGHT 60
END
```

and enter

```
CG PAPER 104 50
```

You can spend many hours finding hundreds upon hundreds of tessellating shapes. If you are familiar with the artwork of M. C. Escher, you have no doubt noticed that he has created numerous tessellating patterns from birds, fish, salamanders, and the like.

Although some patterns cannot be used to fill space, there is no limit to the creation of tessellating patterns once you know the rules.

6 – Stars and Primes

We had the sky, up there, all speckled with stars, and we used to lay on our backs and look up at them and discuss about whether they was made, or only just happened. Mark Twain, *Huckleberry Finn*

Complex Polygons

The Total Turtle Trip Theorem applies to simple polygons—those polygons whose lines don't cross over each other. But this type of polygon is just one of a larger family of figures made from straight lines. Technically, any closed figure made from straight lines is a polygon. A complex polygon (such as that shown) obeys another form of the total trip theorem, which we will develop later in this chapter.

One type of complex polygon that is quite beautiful is the star. (We saw one example of a star in the previous chapter.) For example, if you enter

```
CG REPEAT 5 [FORWARD 100 RIGHT 144]
```

you will have a five-pointed star on the screen.

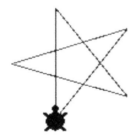

Stars and Primes

Next, let's create another five-sided figure—a regular pentagon. Enter

```
REPEAT 5 [FORWARD 100 RIGHT 72]
```

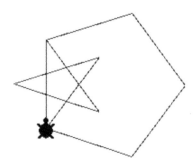

The only difference in the instructions that drew these figures is that we turned 144 degrees after drawing each line on the star and 72 degrees after drawing each line on the pentagon. To draw a star, we doubled the angle we used to draw a pentagon. If we were to write the instructions for drawing a pentagon this way:

```
REPEAT 5 [FORWARD 100 RIGHT (360 / 5)]
```

then we would write the instructions for a five-pointed star this way:

```
REPEAT 5 [FORWARD 100 RIGHT (360 * 2 / 5)]
```

[NOTE: Lynx uses the asterisk (*) to denote multiplication.]

Clear the screen and use the previous two commands to see how they work.

Let's see if the key to making a star from any simple polygon involves simply doubling the turning angle. Enter

```
CG REPEAT 6 [FORWARD 100 RIGHT (360 / 6)]
```

to draw a hexagon. Then enter the following command to see if it produces a six-pointed star:

```
CG REPEAT 6 [FORWARD 100 RIGHT (360 * 2 / 6)]
```

Instead of drawing a star, the second instruction drew a triangle.

Stars and Relatively Prime Numbers

To find out which turning angles produce stars and which do not, it would be useful to have a procedure that lets us try patterns out quickly. The procedure we seek is similar to POLY, except that it has a multiplier that needs to be specified. Here is one way to write this procedure:

```
TO STAR :MULT :SIDES
REPEAT :SIDES [FORWARD 100 RIGHT (360 * :MULT /
:SIDES)]
END
```

(Note the space after the division sign!)

Test this procedure by entering

```
CG STAR 1 5
```

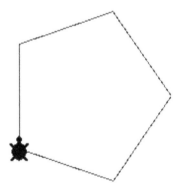

This should draw a simple regular pentagon on the screen. If you then enter

```
STAR 2 5
```

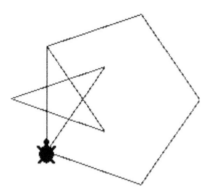

you should see a five-pointed star as well.

To see why some combinations of multipliers and sides produce stars while others do not, let's examine some patterns based on nine-sided polygons. Enter

```
CG STAR 1 9
```

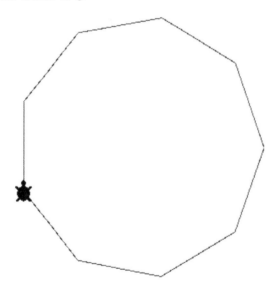

to draw a simple nonagon.

Then enter

STAR 2 9

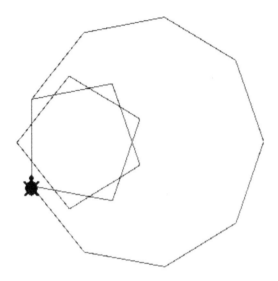

The last command generated a nine-pointed star. Next, let's change the multiplier to 3 and see what happens:

STAR 3 9

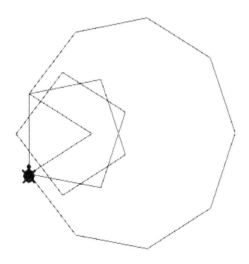

This last command generated a triangle.

To organize our search for star-producing combinations of multipliers and sides, we can make a table with this heading:

STAR TABLE

Multiplier	Sides	Star? (Y or N)

In the first two columns, we will put the values we try for various multipliers and numbers of sides; then we will note what kind of figure each combination produces.

In creating these patterns, we need to know the limit for trial values of the multiplier. Suppose that we choose a multiplier whose value is the same as the number of sides in the polygon. In this case the turtle would turn 360 degrees at the end of each line, and the figure would never close. Thus we see that we must limit our multiplier to a value less than the number of sides.

For our purposes, we won't have to use multipliers whose value is greater than half the number of sides. To see why, let's experiment with various seven-sided polygons. To keep the screen uncluttered, you might wish to clear the screen after generating each of the figures.

CG STAR 1 7

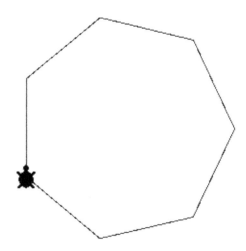

CG STAR 2 7

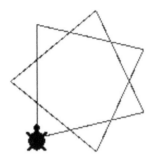

CG STAR 3 7

CG STAR 4 7

CG STAR 5 7

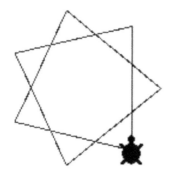

CG STAR 6 7

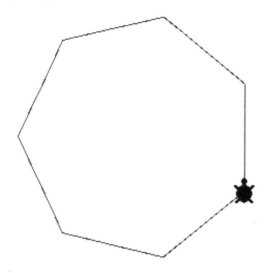

If we look carefully at the six polygons we just drew, we can see that STAR 6 7 produced a mirror image of the regular heptagon drawn by STAR 1 7.

Other mirror images can be seen in the figures drawn by STAR 2 7 and STAR 5 7 and in those drawn by STAR 3 7 and STAR 4 7. As we use multipliers greater than half the number of sides, we generate mirror images of the preceding patterns in reverse order until we once again create the simple regular polygon.

Since no new patterns are generated when we use numbers larger than half the number of sides, this simplifies our task in filling out the star table. In filling out your copy of the table, remember that our goal is the production of stars with the same number of points as the number of drawn sides. There were two such stars for the heptagon—one with a multiplier of 2 and another with a multiplier of 3.

The following table shows the results for polygons with up to 11 sides:

STAR TABLE

Multiplier	Sides	Star? (Y or N)
2	4	N
2	5	Y
2	6	N
3	6	N
2	7	Y
3	7	Y
2	8	N
3	8	Y
4	8	N
2	9	Y
3	9	N
4	9	Y
2	10	N
3	10	Y
4	10	N (5-pointed)
5	10	N
2	11	Y
3	11	Y
4	11	Y
5	11	Y

We did not include a multiplier of 1 in the table because we already know that we will get a simple polygon with that value.

As we look at this table, we see many yeses and many noes. Let's look more closely to see if there is a pattern to these results. First let's see if there are any polygons for which all multipliers (greater than 1) give a star. We can see that when the number of sides is equal to 5, 7, or 11, all values of multipliers produce stars! The numbers 5, 7, and 11 are prime numbers, numbers that cannot be formed by the multiplication of two whole numbers, both of which must be greater than 1. The number 6 is not a prime number, since 6 is 2 * 3; the numbers 2 and 3 are the factors of 6. The number 7, however, cannot be written as the product of two whole numbers, so it is a prime number.

So far, we have discovered that polygons whose number of sides equals a prime number can be turned into stars for any multiplier other than 1 or number of sides less 1. But what about numbers like 8? When we look at polygons with eight sides, we find that some multipliers give stars and others don't. Let's look at this more closely. With eight-sided polygons, multipliers of 2 or 4 don't produce stars, but a multiplier of 3 does. Now it so happens that both 2 and 4 are factors of 8. We do get a star when we use 3, but 3 is not a factor of 8. When we consider nine-sided polygons, we see the same sort of thing. In any particular case, if the multiplier and the number of sides have a common factor, we will not get a star with the same number of points as drawn sides. We can thus create a rule for stars:

A polygon with S sides can be turned into a star with S points by increasing each turning angle by M times, when M is a whole number that shares no factors with S.

Before concluding this chapter, we should revisit the total trip theorem. For simple closed figures, the turtle always turns a total of 360 degrees. For the five pointed star (STAR 2 5), the total turning angle was 720 degrees (2 * 360). For the two seven-pointed stars, the turning angles were 720 degrees and 1080 degrees (3 * 360), respectively. Notice that as the total turning angle increases, the lines of the star move closer to the center of the figure.

We can now rephrase the total trip theorem to cover any polygon:

For any closed figure, the total turning angle will be N* 360, where N is an integer greater than or equal to 1.

7 – Procedures Using Procedures

To see a World in a Grain of Sand
And Heaven in a Wild Flower
Hold Infinity in the palm of your hand
And Eternity in an hour
– William Blake, *Auguries of Innocence*

Thus far we have learned, among other things, how to extend Lynx by the creation of procedures. In this chapter we will explore, among other things, the ability of procedures to use other procedures.

To start with a simple example, suppose that we want to draw a five-pointed star. We can do this using the STAR procedure described in the previous chapter. After making certain that the procedure is in the Lynx workspace, enter

```
CG STAR 2 5
```

Now suppose that we want to draw this same star each time we use another word—PENTAGRAM, for example. To do that we can create the procedure

```
TO PENTAGRAM
STAR 2 5
END
```

If we now relocate the turtle by entering

```
PENUP SETPOS [120 0] PENDOWN
```

and enter

```
PENTAGRAM
```

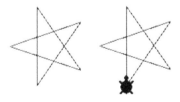

we will see a second identical star on the screen.

The procedure PENTAGRAM uses the procedure STAR. One of Lynx's features is that procedures can use each other and can even pass variables to each other. For example, suppose you grew tired of entering the word STAR each time and wanted to be able to just enter a single letter, S. This procedure will accomplish this task for you:

```
TO S :MULT :SIDES
STAR :MULT :SIDES
END
```

Now you can create a star by using either S or STAR. In other words, S 7 15 generates the same figure as STAR 7 15, because both commands ultimately use the same STAR procedure.

As you experiment some more with this idea, try creating a procedure that uses STAR but reverses the order of the inputs. This procedure—let's call it T—has the property that T 14 3 generates the same figure as STAR 3 14.

Windmills and Flower Blossoms

We are now in a position to develop some new procedures that use some old procedures (such as POLY) to explore some aspects of rotational symmetry. If you have not already done so, you should make sure that POLY is in your Lynx workspace.

Some very nice patterns can be made by taking a simple object and repeating it at equal angles around the center of the screen. Because of the flowerlike patterns that often result, we will call the procedure that does this FLOWER.

FLOWER needs two pieces of information to do its job. First, it needs to know how many times to repeat the pattern around the center of the screen, and then it needs a list of instructions for generating the pattern to be repeated. We already know that in a procedure like STAR, the command STAR 2 5 will cause the numbers 2 and 5 to be passed to the appropriate places of the procedure definition so they can be used. Lynx variables can be numbers, words, or lists. If we want to pass a series of Lynx instructions to a procedure, the easiest way is to pass them as a list. This means that we would bundle the instructions together and enclose them in square brackets. (The Lynx command REPEAT operates this way.) To draw eight pentagons around the screen, we might enter FLOWER 8 [POLY 40 5]. The value of the first variable is the number 8 and the value of the second variable is a list containing the instructions POLY 40 5.

Once an instruction list is passed to a procedure, we need to be able to instruct Lynx to run the instructions. After all, the elements in the list might be just words, they might be the names of variables, or, as in this case, they might be a sequence of Lynx commands. To run a list containing Lynx commands, we use the RUN command. The command RUN is always followed by a list containing a series of instructions made of Lynx commands and procedures.

The FLOWER procedure uses RUN in the following way:

```
TO FLOWER :SIDES :INSTRUCTIONLIST
REPEAT :SIDES [RUN :INSTRUCTIONLIST
RIGHT 360 / :SIDES]
END
```

[NOTE: Remember that our choice of variable names is for our own convenience in remembering what they should contain. We could just as easily have created the procedure as FLOWER :GEORGE :FREDDY.]

Before using this new procedure, it is interesting to compare FLOWER with a similar procedure, POLY:

```
TO POLY :SIZE :SIDES
REPEAT :SIDES [FORWARD SIZE RIGHT 360 / :SIDES]
END
```

The only difference between FLOWER and POLY is that POLY uses the single command FORWARD before turning, whereas FLOWER is set up to use any number of commands before turning. To examine this further, enter

```
CG FLOWER 5 [FORWARD 60]
```

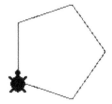

By letting FLOWER use the command FORWARD 60, we drew the same pentagon we would have drawn with POLY 60 5.

FLOWER is much more general than POLY, however, since we can use any combination of commands in place of FORWARD.

As an example, let's try the following:

```
CG FLOWER 5 [FORWARD 40 REPEAT 5 [FORWARD 30 RIGHT
144]]
```

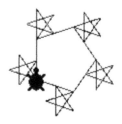

This procedure generated a pattern of five stars on the corners of a pentagon.

We should make note of the fact that FLOWER has thus far produced closed figures. Is this always the case? We can show that it is not by example:

```
CG FLOWER 5 [FORWARD 40 LEFT 30]
```

The reason this figure is not closed is that the turtle did not turn a net multiple of 360 degrees in generating the figure. FLOWER will always create closed figures so long as the procedures and commands in INSTRUCTIONLIST leave the turtle pointing in the same direction it was pointing at the beginning of the commands. In other words, if the net turning in INSTRUCTIONLIST is zero or a multiple of 360 degrees, FLOWER will always generate a closed figure.

For example, enter

```
CG FLOWER 7 [FORWARD 20 LEFT 60 FORWARD 20 RIGHT 120
FORWARD 20 LEFT 60 FORWARD 20]
```

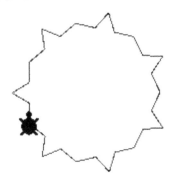

The commands FORWARD 20 LEFT 60 FORWARD 20 RIGHT 120 FORWARD 20 LEFT 60 FORWARD 20 have a net turning angle of zero, and the resulting figure is closed.

Aside from generating some interesting patterns, FLOWER can let us explore some aspects of rotational symmetry. For example, suppose that we create a pentagon by using

```
CG POLY 50 5
```

This figure has fivefold rotational symmetry. If we now create a flower pattern from this pentagon by entering

```
FLOWER 8 [POLY 50 5]
```

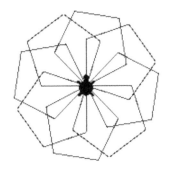

We have generated a new figure that has eightfold rotational symmetry.

In other words, FLOWER creates a figure whose rotational symmetry is determined by the number of rotations made by FLOWER, not by the symmetry of the repeated pattern used by FLOWER.

Each of the following commands generates a figure with eightfold symmetry, even though the individual elements that are repeated have threefold, fourfold, fivefold, or sixfold rotational symmetry. (You. may wish to clear the screen before drawing each of these patterns.)

FLOWER 8 [POLY 50 3]

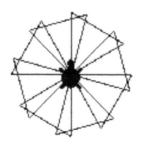

FLOWER 8 [POLY 50 4]

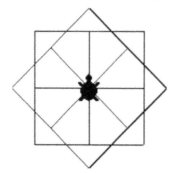

FLOWER 8 [POLY 50 5]

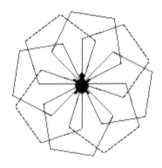

FLOWER 8 [POLY 40 6]

This shows that a pattern of one symmetry can be used as the building block of a pattern with any other symmetry. It is interesting to note that there is no limit to how far this can go. For example, we created a triangle by using

POLY 40 3

This figure has threefold symmetry. Next we used FLOWER with this pattern to generate a figure with eightfold symmetry:

FLOWER 8 [POLY 40 3]

Now we will use FLOWER to repeat this pattern to generate a figure with fivefold symmetry. We do this by having FLOWER use itself. The act of having a procedure use itself is called recursion. Because variable names in Lynx are locally defined within each procedure each time it is used, a procedure can use itself or any other procedures with the same variable names without confusion. Recursion will be covered in far greater detail in a later chapter. For now, just know it is one of the most important (if somewhat counter-intuitive) features of "first-class" languages like Lynx. Meanwhile, to see that it works, enter

```
CG FLOWER 5 [FORWARD 60 FLOWER 8 [POLY 60 3] BACK 60]
```

Notice that we used FORWARD and BACK to move our eightfold pattern off center.

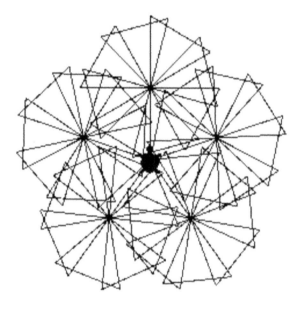

The resulting flower (is it an apple blossom?) has fivefold symmetry and is made from elements with eightfold symmetry that are made from elements with threefold symmetry. The symmetry of the overall figure is determined by the last symmetry operation performed.

8 – Angles, Squares, and Squirals

What comes out of all this is that a spiral is a figure that retains its shape (i.e., proportion) as it grows in one dimension by addition at the open end. You see, there are no truly static spirals.
– Gregory Bateson, *Mind and Nature*

Thus far, we have explored graphic procedures that produce static images. In looking at their finished form, there is no clue to the process that created them. In this chapter, we will explore some classes of geometric figures that are formed by a sequential growth process. Generally, this means that we will be dealing with a set of commands that are repeated to form the object. By increasing the size of the lines drawn with each repetition of the command sequence, an object is caused to grow on the display screen. Lynx provides us with several ways to perform this task. Central to each of them is the concept of a counter.

Suppose that we want to create a procedure that types out the sequence of numbers 0, 1, 2, 3, ... How would we do this? We could use a variable to store the number we are counting, but we need to know how to have Lynx change this number each time it is used. One way to make a counter is to place the starting number in a variable (using the MAKE command) and add one to the old value. For example, consider the following counter procedure:

```
TO COUNTER1 :VALUE
SHOW :VALUE
MAKE 'VALUE' :VALUE + 1
COUNTER1 :VALUE
END
```

If you try this procedure by entering

```
COUNTER1 0
```

your screen will display a column of numbers starting from 0 and continuing upward in increments of one. We did not provide any way for COUNTER1 to stop. This procedure lets us be like the sorcerer's apprentice in Walt Disney's Fantasia, who started having a broom to do his chores for him but couldn't stop it when it got out of control. To stop the counter, click your mouse on the circle with the embedded square on the left side of the Command pane.

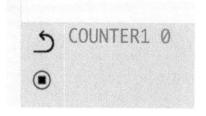

The procedure COUNTER1 is but one of many ways of making a counter. There is a shorter way that might seem to be a little harder to understand. Enter the procedure

```
TO COUNTER2 :VALUE
SHOW :VALUE
COUNTER2 :VALUE + 1
END
```

If you now enter COUNTER2 0, you will see that it behaves similarly to COUNTER1. The secret to COUNTER2 is the third line. When this procedure uses itself again, the number that is passed to the next use of VALUE: the old value plus one. We will see more examples of this type of parameter passing in a later chapter. For our purposes, the explicit use of the MAKE command is perhaps easier to understand.

When making a counter, it is often a good idea to have it stop when it reaches a preset limit. What we want is to have the procedure use itself over and over again, so long as the number counted is not greater than the limit. Lynx provides ways to test for certain conditions and to do something on the basis of the results. The technique we will explore uses the IF command. Structurally, this command takes the form:

IF predicate list

A Lynx predicate is a special word or expression that is either true or false. Suppose that we want to test if a number stored in the variable VALUE is greater than 100. In Lynx we would write

IF :VALUE > 100 list

[NOTE: The symbols <, =, and > are used to compare two numbers to see if the first is less than, equal to, or greater than the second, respectively.]

After the predicate, the Lynx IF command needs a list of commands to be executed in the event that the predicate is true. The list can be as short as one command, or it can be several commands long. In any case, the list (as all Lynx lists) must be enclosed in square brackets. If the tested predicate is not true, the list will be ignored and Lynx will proceed to the next line in the procedure. For our counter application, we want the procedure to stop execution when the predicate is true. The Lynx command that accomplishes this is STOP. The entire IF statement looks like this:

```
IF :VALUE > 100 [STOP]
```

When Lynx encounters STOP in a procedure, it checks to see if there is any unfinished business in any previous procedures and then returns to the command level.

To see how this works, modify COUNTER1 to make it into COUNTER3, as follows:

```
TO COUNTER3 :VALUE :LIMIT
IF :VALUE > :LIMIT [STOP]
SHOW :VALUE
MAKE "VALUE :VALUE + 1
COUNTER3 :VALUE :LIMIT
END
```

If you then enter

```
COUNTER3 0 50
```

you will see a list of the numbers from 0 to 50. As soon as :VALUE exceeded 50, it failed the test in the IF command, and the procedure stopped. COUNTER3 was used 51 separate times. Since there was nothing left to do in the previous uses of COUNTER3, Lynx returned to the command level.

Another method for making a counter involves the use of the REPEAT command. This is illustrated in the procedure COUNTER4:

```
TO COUNTER4 :VALUE :LIMIT
REPEAT (:LIMIT - :VALUE) [SHOW :VALUE MAKE 'VALUE'
:VALUE + 1]
END
```

[NOTE: Normal parentheses can be used freely to group mathematical operations. This makes the operations easier to read and avoids any possibility of Lynx misinterpreting them.]

The COUNTER4 procedure repeats the counter sequence by an amount given by the difference between the limit and the starting value. Since this is calculated at the very beginning of the procedure, the fact that the contents of VALUE is changed later does not affect the operation of this procedure.

If you now enter

```
COUNTER4 0 50
```

you will get something slightly different from the result you got with COUNTER3. In fact, the counter will stop at 49, since this is the fiftieth number it counted (0 was the first). You should be able to modify COUNTER4 so it will always produce results identical to those of COUNTER3.

In the remainder of this chapter, we will explore ways counters can be used to assist in the creation of growing patterns.

Growing Squares

Using the counter concept, we can let Lynx generate figures by a process of growth. For example, suppose that we create a procedure that generates a square:

```
TO SQUARE :SIZE
REPEAT 4 [FORWARD :SIZE RIGHT 90]
END
```

We can use this procedure inside another procedure that will generate a growing square:

```
TO GROWSQUARE :LIMIT
MAKE 'SIZE' 0
REPEAT :LIMIT [SQUARE :SIZE MAKE 'SIZE' :SIZE + 1]
END
```

If you now enter the commands

```
CG GROWSQUARE 100
```

you will see a solid square grow from a dot at the center of the screen to its final size.

If we want to make a growing open square (rather than an enlarging solid square), we need to erase each square after we draw it and then draw the next larger square. You should be able to modify GROWSQUARE to make this work. An alternative form of this type of growth is illustrated as follows for a five-pointed star (use the STAR procedure you've created before):

```
TO GROWSTAR :SIZE :LIMIT
PENDOWN
STAR :SIZE
IF :SIZE > :LIMIT [STOP]
WAIT 1
PENERASE STAR :SIZE
MAKE "SIZE :SIZE + 1
GROWSTAR :SIZE :LIMIT
END
```

If you then enter

```
CG GROWSTAR 5 120
```

you will see a 5-unit star grow into a 120-unit star. The WAIT command causes the execution of the procedure to wait for a fraction of a second before proceeding. This makes the successive stars easier to see.

Squirals

Even though you could see the growth process of the square and star, there is still no way you could have deduced this process by looking at the final figures.

Living things sometimes leave traces of their growth patterns that can be studied without watching the object grow. Seasonal cycles, for example, produce a series of concentric rings in trees. By counting the rings, one can deduce the age of the tree. A more common growth pattern, found in both plants and animals, is the spiral. The effect of spirals on the eye is so strong that they almost appear to be in motion. The curved spirals seen in snail shells, for example, are so important that we will devote a chapter to them later. The remainder of this chapter is devoted to an examination of spirals made with straight lines. These spirals are called squirals (square spirals), even if the individual shape is not a square.

To start, let's examine a spiral made from straight lines and square (90-degree) corners. To draw a square, we draw the same length line after each turn 90 degrees. To draw a square spiral, we need to increase the length of each side over its previous value. Clearly, we can use a counter to do this. The following procedure will allow us to experiment with squirals containing various turning angles. The increment by which each side grows is chosen to be 2, although you may want to change this value as you experiment.

To create the SQUIRAL procedure, enter

```
TO SQUIRAL :ANGLE
MAKE 'SIDE' 0
REPEAT 100 [FORWARD :SIDE RIGHT :ANGLE MAKE 'SIDE'
:SIDE + 2]
END
```

Then enter

```
CG SQUIRAL 90
```

This will generate a square squiral pattern on the display screen.

On examination, we can see the close relation of this figure to the square. Next, suppose that we were to use an angle close to 90 degrees—89 degrees, for example. Before trying this angle, you should try to visualize the result in your mind. Will the change be small or large?

Once you have made your decision, enter

`CG SQUIRAL 89`

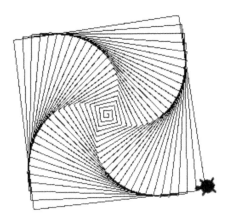

This figure looks quite different from that generated by SQUIRAL 90. Why is this?

As the figure for SQUIRAL 89 is drawn, each turning angle differs from that for a square by only one degree. But the impact of this difference is cumulative as far as the overall figure is concerned. By the time the turtle has made one circuit around the path, the difference is 4 degrees. By the time the procedure stops, the turning angle is 100 degrees in variance from its value for the truly square squiral.

One of the attractions of this figure is the four arching branches twisting to the left. These branches are formed as an interference pattern of corners that bump into each other because of the angular mismatch (compared to a square). Such interferences, called Moiré patterns, are quite common. You can see Moiré patterns by holding two window screens together and rotating one of them slightly with respect to the other. When the screens are adjusted so that there is no interference pattern, the screens are perfectly aligned.

We can see a similar effect with squirals. For example, if we enter

`CG SQUIRAL 91`

we will generate a squiral pattern that has arms branching off to the right.

Whenever we see interference of this sort, it is a clue that we are close to a regular pattern whose alignment of sides creates no interference. If the squirals arch to the left, the angle is too small; if they arch to the right, the angle is too large.

How many squirals are there with no interference patterns? The following figures show examples of squiral patterns based on the pentagon. (You will want to clear the screen before drawing each squiral.)

SQUIRAL 70

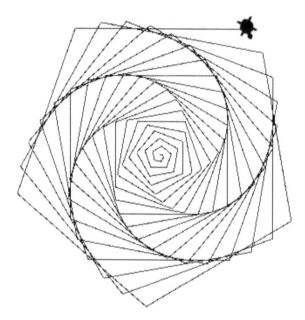

SQUIRAL 71

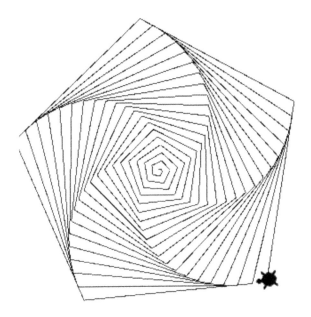

SQUIRAL 72

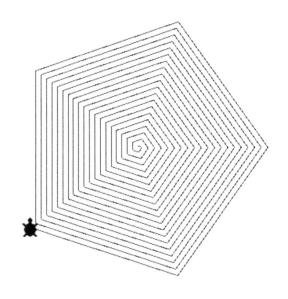

SQUIRAL 73

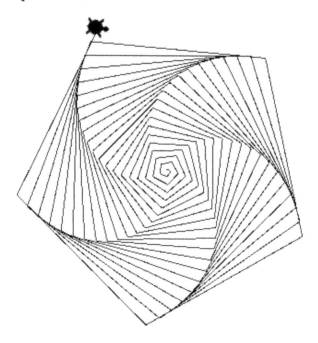

We can see the spiral arms in all patterns except SQUIRAL 72. The 72-degree angle is that associated with a regular pentagon. Notice that the curvature of the spiral arms is greater as you move farther away from 72 degrees in either direction.

The next set of figures explores squirals in the vicinity of 120 degrees:

SQUIRAL 118

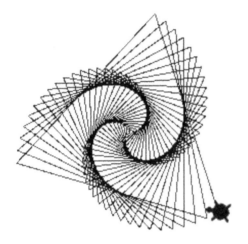

SQUIRAL 119

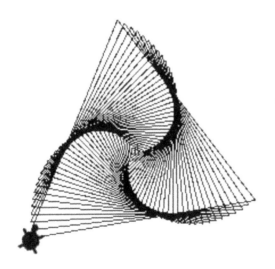

SQUIRAL 120

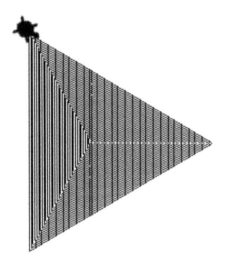

SQUIRAL 121

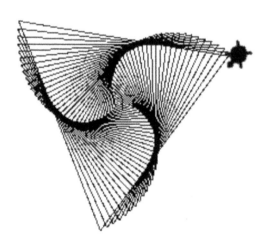

SQUIRAL 122

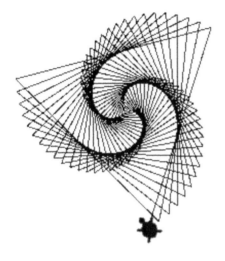

Squiral patterns need not be based on simple polygons. For example, an attractive set of figures occurs in the vicinity of 144 degrees:

SQUIRAL 142

SQUIRAL 143

SQUIRAL 144

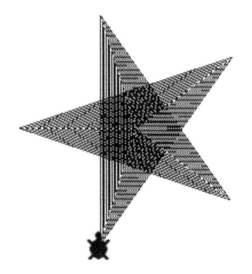

SQUIRAL 145

SQUIRAL 146

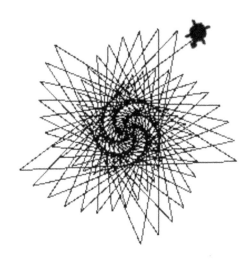

As you experiment with the SQUIRAL procedure, you will find many interesting patterns. Each of these patterns reflects the process of growth by which it was created.

You see, there are no truly static spirals.

9 – Arcs, Circles, and Spirals

Whether the symbol of the circle appears in primitive sun worship or modern religion, in myths or dreams, in the mandalas drawn by the Tibetan monks, in the ground plans of cities, or in the spherical concepts of early astronomers, it always points to the single most vital aspect of life—its ultimate wholeness. – Carl Jung, Man and His Symbols

Thus far, our figures have been made from straight line segments. As pretty as some of these figures are, there are many other figures to be explored that use curved lines.

Central to curved figures is the shape of the circle. Given that Lynx can move forward and can turn (but cannot do both simultaneously), how can we create a procedure to draw a circle?

Circles

One way to create a close approximation to a circle is to draw a short line segment, turn a little, and repeat this process until the figure is closed. Using the total trip theorem, we can tell that our figure will be complete when we have turned 360 degrees.

To try this concept, enter

```
CG REPEAT 360 [FORWARD 1 RIGHT 1]
```

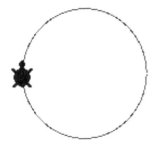

This figure appears to be a circle, but it is really a 360gon. To the limit of the computer's display resolution, however, this polygon is a close enough approximation to a circle for us to call it by that name.

To make smaller circles, we can increase the turning angle. If we turn by a greater amount, the figure will close back on itself more rapidly and thus create a smaller circle. The following procedure lets us test this concept:

```
TO CIRCLE :SIZE :ANGLE
REPEAT 360  / :ANGLE [FORWARD :SIZE RIGHT :ANGLE]
END
```

The reason for making the repeat factor 360 / :ANGLE is to preserve a total turning angle of 360 degrees, as required by the total trip theorem.

To test this new procedure, enter

```
CG CIRCLE 1 1
```

Our display should show the same large circle we drew before. To generate some other circles of different sizes, enter

```
CIRCLE 1 2 CIRCLE 1 3 CIRCLE 1 4 CIRCLE 1 5 CIRCLE 1 6
CIRCLE 1 7 CIRCLE 1 8 CIRCLE 1 9
```

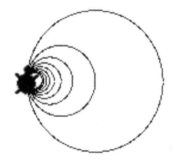

For circles of intermediate sizes, we can use other angular increments, such as 2.5, and the like.

To make an even larger circle than given by CIRCLE 1 1, we could use an angle between 0 and 1 or change the step length from 1 to some other value.

For example, enter the following:

```
CG CIRCLE 2 1 CIRCLE 2 2 CIRCLE 2 3 CIRCLE 2 4 CIRCLE 2
5 CIRCLE 2 6 CIRCLE 2 7 CIRCLE 2 8 CIRCLE 2 9
```

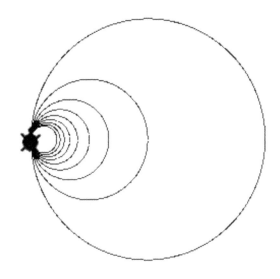

Each circle in this drawing is twice as large as its counterpart in the previous figure. One can easily see the reason for this by measuring the circumference of these circles. The circumference is given by 360 / :ANGLE multiplied by the step size. For a given angle increment, doubling the step size doubles the circumference.

This observation leads to an interesting discovery: Any two circles for which the ratios of step size to angle increment are the same will have the same circumference. To test this, enter the following:

```
CG CIRCLE 1 1 SETC 2 CIRCLE 2 2 SETC 3 CIRCLE 3 3 SETC
4 CIRCLE 4 4 SETC 5 CIRCLE 5 5
```

Since each circle was drawn in a different color, it is easy to see each circle as it overlays its predecessor. Notice that, although the first few circles overlaid each other almost perfectly, the mismatch became more visible when the step size became larger. The reason for this is quite simple. We are creating circular shapes by approximation with polygons. As we increase the turning angle, we are reducing the number of sides in the polygon and thus producing a poorer approximation to a circle.

As an extreme, try the following:

```
CG SETC 'BLACK' CIRCLE 1 1 CIRCLE 45 45 CIRCLE 90 90
```

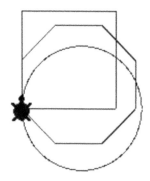

Each of these figures has the same circumference as the others (360 units), yet only the first resembles a circle.

Parts of Circles

Suppose that, instead of forming a complete circle, we wish to create only a portion of the circle—an arc. To do this, we need to have the turtle repeat its sequence of drawing and turning until the desired angle has been reached. For example, these two figures are both 90-degree arcs:

```
CG REPEAT 90 [FORWARD 1 RIGHT 1] PENUP HOME PENDOWN
REPEAT 45 [FORWARD 1 RIGHT 2]
```

Even though these arcs have different sizes, they each comprise one-quarter of a circle. Arcs are useful building blocks for other figures, as we shall see in the next chapter.

In the previous chapter, we created squirals by keeping the turning angle fixed and increasing the size of the drawn lines. By reversing this sequence, we can create some interesting spirals. To make a spiral curve we can draw a series of fixed length lines and turn the turtle by increasing amounts at the end of each step. Using our previous experience with counters, it should not be too difficult to design a spiral procedure.

Rather than starting with such a procedure, we can create a spiral interactively by using primitive Lynx commands. For example, enter

```
CG MAKE 'ANGLE' 0 REPEAT 45 [FORWARD 7 RIGHT :ANGLE
MAKE 'ANGLE' :ANGLE + 1]
```

This set of instructions starts the turtle off on a gentle arc to the right that begins to circle in on itself very quickly.

Next, enter

```
REPEAT 45 [FORWARD 7 RIGHT :ANGLE MAKE 'ANGLE' :ANGLE + 1]
```

This continues to tighten the spiral. If we take an additional 90 steps (making 180 in total) by entering

```
REPEAT 90 [FORWARD 7 RIGHT :ANGLE MAKE 'ANGLE' :ANGLE + 1]
```

Note that I hid the turtle so you could see the spiral shape. This last command will bring the turtle to the center of the circular area that is forming on the screen.

What will happen for angles greater than 180 degrees? When we started, the turtle turned first by 1 degree, then by 2 degrees, and so on. After the first four steps, the turtle had turned by only 10 degrees. Contrast this with the turning that took place at the four steps starting at 89 degrees. After these four steps, the turtle had turned more than 360 degrees. By the time we reached 180-degree increments, the turtle was simply moving back and forth over its position.

To see what happens for increments greater than 180 degrees, enter

```
REPEAT 180 [FORWARD 7 RIGHT :ANGLE MAKE 'ANGLE' :ANGLE + 1]
```

At the end of 360 steps, the turtle is back at the origin, having retraced its steps. Now, however, the turtle is pointing down rather than up.

To complete the figure (and return the turtle to its home position), we need to take an additional 360 steps:

```
REPEAT 360 [FORWARD 7 RIGHT :ANGLE MAKE 'ANGLE' :ANGLE + 1]
```

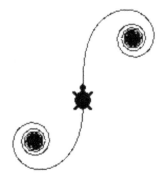

This spiral figure was made by taking 720 steps. The first 360 steps created the upper right arm of the spiral, and the second 360 steps created the lower left arm.

If we were to continue repeating these same commands, we would retrace the original figure. Unlike the squiral patterns, this spiral is a closed figure. Whereas the squiral displays dynamic symmetry, the complete form of this spiral is as static and complete as a simple polygon, such as a square or a triangle.

This type of spiral is but one member of a whole family of such curves. A procedure that lets us create this and other examples of closed spirals is as follows:

```
TO CLOSESPI :SIZE :ANGLE :INCREMENT
 REPEAT 720 [FORWARD :SIZE RIGHT :ANGLE MAKE 'ANGLE'
:ANGLE + :INCREMENT]
END
```

This procedure lets us create figures with different angle increments and with different starting angles. Our previous spiral can be drawn by entering

```
CG CLOSESPI 7 0 1
```

Suppose that, instead of increasing the turning angle in 1-degree steps, we choose another example, 7 degrees. On first thought, we might expect to get a smaller version of the existing spiral, since we have changed only the increment by which the angle is changed. To see what happens, enter

```
CG CLOSESPI 7 0 7
```

This surprising result occurs because the increment was chosen to keep us from reaching a turning angle of 180 degrees in the first arm of the spiral. As a result, the curve could not retrace itself until this condition was met.

More polygonal forms of the spiral can be made by starting with an offset angle. These three figures were made using

```
CLOSESPI 15 40 30
```

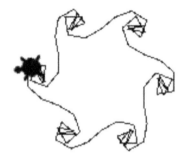

```
CLOSESPI 20 1 20
```

```
CLOSESPI 20 2 20
```

You may wish to experiment some more with this procedure. It can create many beautiful pictures.

Linear or Archimedean spirals

So far, the spirals we generated were different from the kinds of spirals you may be familiar with. For example, if I was to ask you to draw a spiral, you would probably draw something like this,

Or this.

The first of these is called a linear or Archimedean spiral, characterized by each turn being the same distance from the preceding one, kind of like the grooves in a phonograph record. (Ask a grandparent to explain what a phonograph is.)

The second spiral is called a logarithmic spiral often found in sea shells, and is a major topic of the next chapter.

For now, we'll focus on the linear spiral.

Spirals in fine art

Take a look at this picture os Rafael's *Madonna of the chair,* probably painted in 1513 or 1514.

This amazing painting is on display at the Pitti Palace in Florence, Italy. You can see and download a high resolution copy of this image from Wikipedia by searching on Madonna della seggiola (Madonna of the chair).

To my eye, I thought I saw a spiral embedded in this painting. To test this out, I downloaded the image and added it to my Lynx clip art library to use as a background.

To see the clip art library, click on the picture of the house on the left side of the main Lynx screen. This brings up a collection of numbered squares, and of which can hold a piece of clip art.

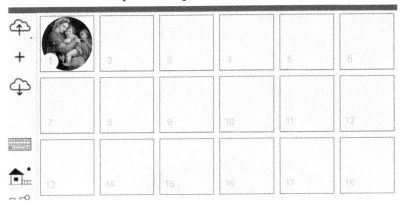

When you click on one of the squares a + sign shows up and you can add a piece of clip art from your computer. In this case, I added the Rafael painting in box 1.

To use this art as a background on your graphics screen, enter the following in the Command pane.

```
CG ST
SETSHAPE 1
STAMP
FREEZEBG
CG
SETSHAPE 0
```

These commands do the following: Clear the screen, show the turtle, set the turtle shape to clip art 1, stamp the image on the screen, freeze the background screen, clear the graphics screen to see that the stamped image stays put, and set the turtle shape to the original shape and size.

Now we can get ready to draw our spiral. We'll start by making the pen width a bit bigger so the line is easier to see. I chose 3. Also, I changed the color to green to contrast with the colors on the painting. Also, I wanted the turtle to start at the infant's elbow, so I moved it up a little bit.

This is all done by entering the following in the Command pane:

```
SETPENSIZE 3
SETC 'GREEN'
PU FD 15 PD
```

Now we are ready to experiment with different spirals.

Create the following procedure:

```
TO SPIRAL :SIZE :INCREMENT
REPEAT 1000 [FD :SIZE RT 1 MAKE 'SIZE' :SIZE +
.:INCREMENT]
END
```

The following image appears when you enter:

```
SPIRAL 0 0.003
```

Note that, starting at the elbow of the infact, the spiral follows the curve of the Madonna's arm, up through the infant's lips, down along the thigh, up through the Madonna's right eye, and through the left eye of John the Baptist and the infant's foot.

Is this a coincidence, or was Rafael consciously incorporating a linear spiral through this amazing painting? In addition to his paintings, he was also an architect, and would have been quite familiar with the kinds of logarithmic spirals we'll explore in the next chapter, but as for the linear spiral shown here, there is no evidence I could find to answer this question one way or the other.

In the next chapter, we will explore other methods for creating spirals, and these spirals will display dynamic symmetry and also some connections to fine art.

10 – The Golden Mean

It may be argued that design may become an intellectual process, but it is just as important for the designer to understand the laws of harmoniously related forms and areas, as it is for the musical composer to be familiar with the laws of harmony and counterpoint.
– Edward B. Edwards, *Pattern and Design with Dynamic Symmetry*

With the single exception of Archimedean spirals, the forms we have studied thus far have displayed static symmetry. In this chapter, we will explore one family of geometric forms that displays a dynamic symmetry based on the golden mean.

The origin of the golden mean is buried in antiquity. There is evidence that it was known to the Greek sculptor Phidias (c. 500 BC) and that it was used as a proportion in the construction of the Parthenon. By the 1500s, its appearance in mathematics became so commonplace that a book on the topic was published by Luca Pacioli (issuu.com/s.c.williams-library/docs/de_divina_proportione), with illustrations by Leonardo da Vinci. Since that time, numerous books and articles have been devoted to the appearance of the golden mean in nature and art.

The concept of the golden mean is quite simple: Divide a line into two segments so that the ratio of the longer to the shorter is the same as the ratio of the entire line to the longer segment. This ratio is the golden mean.

If we say that the shorter length is *b* unit long and that the longer segment is *a* units long, then the mathematical expression for the golden mean is

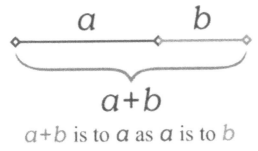

$a+b$ is to a as a is to b

$$\frac{a+b}{a} = \frac{a}{b} \, defines \, \phi$$

Where *phi* (ϕ) commonly represents the Golden Mean. It is an irrational number that is the positive root to the quadratic equation:

$$x^2 - x - 1 = 0$$

which produces the result:

$$\phi = \frac{\sqrt{5}+1}{2} \approx 1.61803$$

The golden mean has the property that, when diminished by 1, it becomes its own reciprocal. In other words,

1.61803 ... = 1/0.61803....

The golden mean is a number that appears to demonstrate an affinity for itself. It is as though, once you have it, nothing you do to it will make it go away.

You'll probably end up using the Golden Mean so much that it would be nice to have it as an available constant. Lynx already has PI, so let's add to the collection with PHI.

```
TO PHI
OUTPUT (((SQRT 5) + 1) / 2)
END
```

The common OUTPUT is used in a procedure to give a value and then stop the procedure. Once you have this available, you can use it anywhere you'd use the numeric approximation, 1.61803. In the remainder of this chapter, I'll use the numeric approximation, but the choice is up to you. Also PHI requires less typing!

The Magic Rectangle

Recall that we said that a figure displaying dynamic symmetry could be extended by applying the same rules that generated the figure in the first place. To see a graphic example of this phenomenon for the golden mean, we will start by constructing a golden rectangle—one whose length is 1.61803... times longer than its height.

Rectangles with this aspect ratio often are spontaneously selected as being the most pleasing to the eye. Why our aesthetic sense should lead to this conclusion is a mystery. (You can test this result for yourself by constructing a series of rectangles ranging from a square to a rectangle with a ratio of 2:1 and asking people to select the most pleasing shape.)

Suppose that we say that the height of the rectangle is 1 unit. Its length is then 1.61803... units. If we now draw a 1-unit square in this rectangle, we see that another rectangle is left over.

The short side of this rectangle is 0.61803... units, and the long side is 1 unit. The ratio of the long to the short side is 1/0.61803..., or the golden mean. In other words, if we subtract a square from a golden rectangle, we are left with another golden rectangle for a remainder. This process can be repeated indefinitely, with no change in the result.

The properties of this rectangle were studied by Jay Hambidge in the 1920s. He called it "the rectangle of the whirling squares." The following procedure will show why this name is so appropriate.

To create a procedure that generates a square we can write

```
TO SQUARE :SIZE
REPEAT 4 [FORWARD :SIZE RIGHT 90]
END
```

This generates a square that returns the turtle to its starting position.

To add on to this figure, we need to move the turtle to an edge of the square. For the figure we desire, we need to move the turtle to the upper right corner and have it face to the right. This is most easily done by drawing the first two sides of the square over again.

Once we have moved the turtle to this new position, we want to draw another square that has sides 0.61803... times smaller than the first square. As this procedure is repeated over and over again, we will generate the rectangle of the whirling squares.

```
TO WHIRL :SIZE
IF :SIZE < 1 [STOP]
REPEAT 4 [FORWARD :SIZE RIGHT 90]
FORWARD :SIZE RIGHT 90 FORWARD :SIZE
WHIRL :SIZE * 0.61803
END
```

As you can see, this procedure uses itself over and over again recursively, with each new square being smaller than the previous one by a factor of 0.61803...

To see the whirling squares, enter

```
CG PENUP SETPOS [-120 -60] PENDOWN WHIRL 300
```

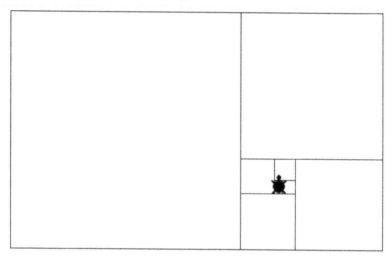

Next, imagine drawing a 90-degree arc connecting the two opposite corners of each square. As these arcs connect, they produce a spiral.

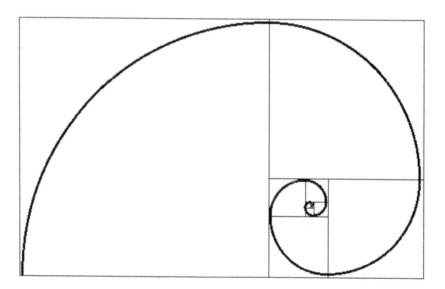

The proportional rule behind this spiral is that each segment is larger than its predecessor by the golden mean. Hint: If you want to draw this spiral, you'll need to modify the LSPIRAL procedure we'll soon explore. The modification is a small change in the starting size,, but very much worth your effort

Spirals that grow by fixed ratios are common in nature. They appear in snail shells, whirlpools, and numerous other natural objects and phenomena. Because of the various mathematical properties of such spirals, the same spiral can be called by different names. For example, because the angle at which the radius vector cuts the curve at any point is a constant, Descartes called it an equiangular spiral in 1638. Because of the proportional increase in its size, it has been called a proportional or geometric spiral. Bernoulli (who was so entranced by this figure that he had it engraved on his headstone in 1705) called it a logarithmic spiral. No matter what it is called, however, these names all refer to the same figure.

Spirals of this type can be approximated by a procedure that draws a series of 90-degree arcs for which each arc is larger than its predecessor by a fixed factor. There are two types of spirals—those that turn to the left and those that turn to the right. To generate a right-handed 90-degree arc, we can use the procedure

```
TO RARC :SIZE
REPEAT 30 [FORWARD :SIZE RIGHT 3]
END
```

And we can use this procedure for generating right handed spirals by creating the procedure

```
TO RSPIRAL :STEPS :FACTOR
MAKE 'SIZE' 0.1
REPEAT :STEPS [RARC :SIZE MAKE 'SIZE' :SIZE  * :FACTOR]
END
```

To generate left-handed spirals, we would use the procedures

```
TO LARC :SIZE
REPEAT 30 [FORWARD :SIZE LEFT 3]
END

TO LSPIRAL :STEPS :FACTOR
MAKE "SIZE 0.1
REPEAT :STEPS [LARC :SIZE MAKE 'SIZE' :SIZE  * :FACTOR]
END
```

Next, we can experiment with spirals that use different expansion factors. If you enter

```
CG  RSPIRAL 10 1
```

all you will see is a dot at the center of the screen. This is because you cannot increase the size of anything by multiplying it by 1. To see a spiral based on the golden mean, enter

```
CG RSPIRAL 15 1.61803
```

By increasing the size of the expansion factor, we can create spirals that are more open. For example, enter

```
CG RSPIRAL 10 2
```

To make a more tightly closed spiral, use numbers closer to 1, such as 1.2:

```
CG RSPIRAL 35 1.2
```

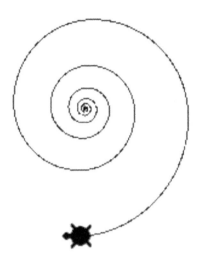

Interlaced spirals can be made by turning the turtle by different amounts before starting the spiral. For example, enter

```
CG LSPIRAL 10 1.5
```

This draws a left-handed spiral from the center of the screen. Next, we will change the pen color to blue and draw the same spiral from the center, but we will first turn the turtle by 180 degrees. Enter

```
PENUP HOME PENDOWN SETCOLOUR 'BLUE' RIGHT 180 LSPIRAL
10 1.5
```

blue

Notice that the blue spiral lies near the middle of the gap in the black spiral. To produce interwoven spirals with different locations, the same process can be repeated with other starting angles. The following example will add an orange line on either side of the blue one:

```
SETCOLOUR 'ORANGE' PENUP HOME PENDOWN RIGHT 90 LSPIRAL
10 1.5 PENUP HOME PENDOWN LEFT 90 LSPIRAL 10 1.5
```

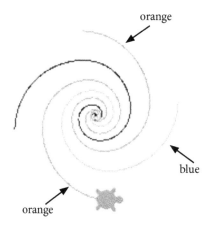

orange

blue

orange

The Mona Lisa

In the previous chapter we explored the linear spiral in one of Raphael's paintings. Now we'll look for a spiral based on the Golden Mean in one of Leonardo da Vinci's most famous paintings, the Mona Lisa

This is probably the most valuable painting in the world and was painted in the early 1500s. For our purposes, we'll look for a Golden Spiral in this painting, encouraged by the fact that the Golden Mean appears in many of Leonardo's works.

We'll put the image in the second position in our Lynx clip art library and in the command pane enter:

```
CG
SETSHAPE 2
STAMP
FREEZEBG
SETSHAPE 0
SETPENSIZE 3
SETCOLOUR 'GREEN'
```

The last **FREEZEBG** command freezes the image in place so it won't go away when we issue the **CG** command. As with the Raphael picture, we reset the pen to the turtle shape, set the pen width to 3, and the color to green.

Now we can experiment. Let's start by placing the Turtle over her lips: It appears that just moving the Turtle forward by 106 should do it. You'll likely need different values for your starting position depending on the copy of the Mona Lisa you are using.

```
CG PU FD 106 LT 90 FD 15 PD
RT 90
LSPIRAL 11 1.61803
```

Now let's make a right-handed Golden Spiral

You'll want to experiment yourself, changing the starting size for example.

Here's the procedure I used:

```
TO LSPIRAL :STEPS :FACTOR
MAKE 'SIZE' 0.085
REPEAT :STEPS [LARC :SIZE MAKE 'SIZE' :SIZE * :FACTOR]
END
```

You'll see that the curve follows the hairline on her left side, and goes down over her right hand.

Of course the real question is whether this fitting of the spiral was intentional or accidental. I'm sure you'll find a variety of opinions on this topic online!

If anything, you should experiment with other artwork to see the use of the Golden Rectangle, and Golden Spiral.

The Magic of Numbers and Fibonacci

Numerical series based on the golden mean were developed by the twelfth-century mathematician Leonardo Bigallo Fibonacci (also known as Leonardo da Pisa). In his travels to Algiers with his father, he learned about the golden mean and also learned the arabic numbering system, which he introduced to Europe, and we still use today.

The numerical series that bears his name is a simple additive series. Each number in the series is formed by adding the previous two numbers in the series. The Fibonacci series starts with the seed numbers 1 and 1. The first few numbers of this series are 1 1 2 3 5 8 13 21 34 55, and so on.

One startling aspect of this series is its spontaneous appearance in nature. It is found, for example, in the interlocking spiral patterns of pinecones and sunflower seed clusters. In these and other plant-based structures, one can discern a set of right-handed and left-handed spiral arms. What is found is that the number of right- and left-handed arms are always two adjacent numbers in the Fibonacci series.

For example, the following procedure creates the kind of pattern you might find in a sunflower seed cluster. This procedure stamps large dots on the screen, rotating by the "Golden Angle" and increasing it's distance from the origin by the square root of the dot number.

The Golden Angle

In our case, we'll explore a related number—the Golden Angle. This is found when a circle is divided into two arcs so the ratio of the circumference to the longer arc equals the ratio of the longer arc to the shorter one. The Golden Angle is the angle subtended by the shorter arc (*b*).

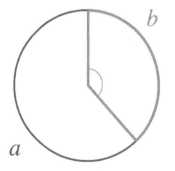

$$360 \left(1 - \tfrac{1}{\phi}\right) \approx 137.508^{\circ}$$

Our next task is to create a Lynx procedure to make a bunch of "sunflower seeds" as they might appear in a flower. This angle will play a critical role!

To draw a model of a seed cluster, we'll start with a square dot centered at the turtle's location:

```
TO DOT :SIZE
SETPENSIZE :SIZE
PU BK :SIZE / 2
PD FD :SIZE
PU BK :SIZE / 2
END
```

Next, let's define a procedure that places these dots on the screen where each dot is placed a distance from the center proportional to the square root of the distance from the center, and rotated around the center by the Golden Angle. The use of the square root of the distance from the center is to keep the density of dots constant.

```
TO SEEDS :INDEX :LIMIT
IF :INDEX > :LIMIT [STOP]
RIGHT 137.508
PU FD (10 * SQRT :INDEX)
PD DOT 5
PU BK (10 * SQRT :INDEX)
SEEDS :INDEX + 1 :LIMIT
END
```

If we use a dot size of 5 and execute

```
CG HT SEEDS 0 250
```

we get the following image:

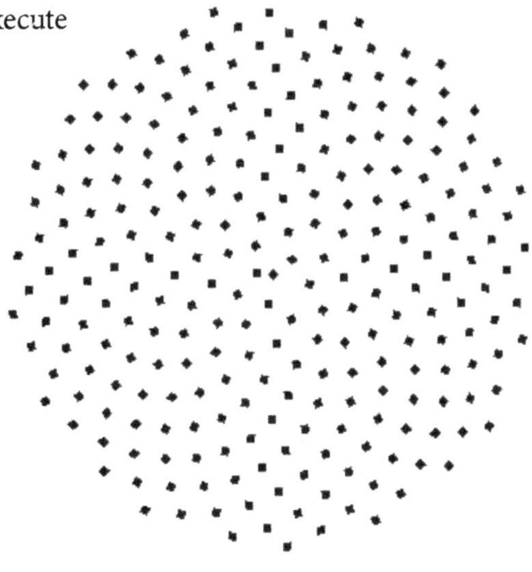

Note that we only placed the dots along a single spiral based on the Golden Angle, yet the image shows two groups of spirals—one set turning to the right, and the other turning to the left. Furthermore, as I mentioned before, the number of each spiral represents two adjacent Fibonacci numbers!

By Stan Shebs, CC BY-SA 3.0, https://commons.wikimedia.org/w/index.php?curid=925941

This natural phenomenon is called *phyllotaxis*.

Why does this pattern show up in so many living organisms? Is it genetic? Do some online researching of your own to find out.

To see another amazing property of the Fibonacci series, we will first develop a Lynx procedure that generates a list of Fibonacci numbers as long as we like. To do this, we must first understand some of the Lynx primitives that work with words and lists. For example, suppose that we create a list:

```
MAKE 'ANIMALS' [DOG CAT HORSE COW]
```

If we want to see the last item in the list, we can use the SHOW command to print results on the Command pane. For example, enter

SHOW LAST :ANIMALS

and see the word COW on the screen. To see the first item in the list, we enter

SHOW FIRST :ANIMALS

We can see all but the last item or all but the first item by entering

SHOW BUTLAST :ANIMALS

or

SHOW BUTFIRST :ANIMALS

The commands FIRST, LAST, BUTFIRST, and BUTLAST can thus be used to take lists apart.

Lists can be put together in Lynx by use of the SENTENCE command. For example, if we have a new animal, SHEEP, saved in the variable MORE:

MAKE 'MORE' 'SHEEP'

we can then add SHEEP to the list ANIMALS in this way:

MAKE 'ANIMALS' SENTENCE :ANIMALS :MORE

If you now enter

SHOW :ANIMALS

you will see the list

DOG CAT HORSE COW SHEEP

Using these commands, we can develop a strategy for building a series. We start with a seed series of at least two numbers and make a new number by adding the last number of the series to the next-to-last number. Finally, we extend the series by placing our new number at the very end of the seed. A two-member seed list will become a three-member list. Since we will want this new list to be the next seed, we need to be able to send its contents back out of the procedure. This is accomplished with the OUTPUT command. If a Lynx procedure encounters a command such as

OUTPUT :SEED

then the current contents of the variable SEED is passed back out of the procedure, and the procedure stops execution.

If these concepts appear a bit vague, our example should help to clarify them. First, we will create a procedure that extends an additive series by one element each time it is used. Enter the following:

```
TO SERIES :SEED
MAKE 'NEXT' (LAST :SEED) + (LAST BUTLAST :SEED)
MAKE 'SEED' SENTENCE :SEED :NEXT
OUTPUT :SEED
END
```

To see what this procedure does, let's trace its execution line by line. First, the contents of NEXT are made to be the sum of the last element in SEED plus the next-to-last element (LAST BUTLAST :SEED). We used parentheses here to make sure that Lynx would perform the operations properly and to make this line easier to read. Next, we place a new list in SEED, made from the old list with the new value (:NEXT) tagged on at the end. Finally, the modified list is passed back out of the procedure by the OUTPUT command.

To try this procedure, enter

```
SHOW SERIES [1 1 2]
```

the display will show

```
1 1 2 3
```

We can use the REPEAT command to build a Fibonacci series of any length. For example, if you enter

```
MAKE 'FSERIES' [1 1] REPEAT 20 [MAKE 'FSERIES' SERIES
:FSERIES]
```

you will build 20 more terms into the series. To see the result, enter

```
SHOW :FSERIES
```

You should see the following list:

```
1 1 2 3 5 8 13 21 34 55 89 144 233 377 610 987 1597
2584 4181 6765 10946 17711
```

So far, we have found a way to build very long lists with numbers of the Fibonacci series. Next, we will do an experiment—dividing the last term in the series by the next-to-last term to see what we get. Here is a procedure that will do this for us:

```
TO RATIO :LIST
OUTPUT (LAST :LIST) / (LAST BUTLAST :LIST)
END
```

If we now enter

```
MAKE 'FSERIES' [1 1] REPEAT 20 [MAKE 'FSERIES' SERIES
:FSERIES] SHOW RATIO :FSERIES
```

we will see the number 1.618034 typed on the screen! This number is the golden mean (to the accuracy of the computer's ability to perform calculations). Is this an accident? Let's expand the list some more-say, by ten more terms:

```
REPEAT 10 [MAKE 'FSERIES' SERIES :FSERIES] SHOW RATIO
:FSERIES
```

1.618034

Once again we are presented, as if by magic, with the golden mean.

Of course, this doesn't hold for all terms in the series. For example, the ratio of the first two terms is 1:1, that of the third to the second is 2:1, and so on. This graph shows the ratios of successive elements for the first ten terms of the Fibonacci series.

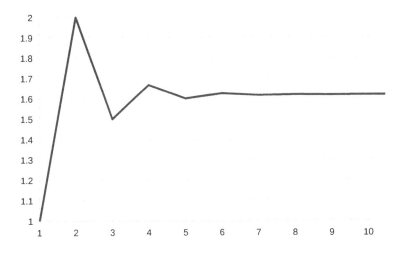

There are two interesting things to notice in this plot. First, the values of each ratio oscillate on either side of the golden mean. Second, the value of the ratio converges very quickly to a value very close to the golden mean.

Even though Fibonacci himself certainly knew about the Golden Ratio, he failed to make the connection between his numbers and the Golden Mean. It wasn't until Johannes Kepler explored these numbers in 1611, almost 400 years after Fibonacci published his work, that Kepler's proof was offered that the ratio of successive Fibonacci numbers approached the Golden Mean. As Kepler said,

> Geometry has two great treasures; one is the Theorem of Pythagoras; the other, the division of a line into extreme and mean ratio. The first we may compare to a measure of gold, the second we may name a precious jewel. — Johannes Kepler

The proof is fairly simple. The goal is to show that:

$$\lim_{n \to \infty} \frac{F_n}{F_{n-1}} = \phi$$

Since the ratio approaches a constant, then it is also the case that (for sufficiently large values of n):

$$\frac{F_n}{F_{n-1}} \approx \frac{F_{n-1}}{F_{n-2}}$$

Since

$$F_n = F_{n-1} + F_{n-2}$$

Then

$$\frac{F_{n-1} + F_{n-2}}{F_{n-1}} \approx \frac{F_{n-1}}{F_{n-2}}$$

Does this look familiar? Remember that the definition of the Golden Mean is:

$$\frac{a+b}{a} = \frac{a}{b}$$

For large values of n these two ratios are nearly the same, proving that the ratio of two successive Fibonacci numbers approaches the Golden Mean as n approaches ∞.

11 – How Long Is the Coast of California? Fractals and Recursion

As I was going to St. Ives, I met a man with seven wives. Each wife carried seven sacks; And in each sack was seven cats; And with each cat was seven kits. Kits, cats, sacks, and wives, How many were going to St. Ives? – Nursery Rhyme

How Long Is a Coastline?

This chapter deals with what appears to be a very simple question: How long is a coastline? One way to measure a coastline would be to use a map and a pair of dividers. Let's say that the map has a scale of one kilometer (km) of actual distance for each centimeter (cm) of distance on the map. If the dividers were set at a 10 cm spacing, a first approximation to the coast length could be obtained by counting the number of 10 cm steps along the coastline shown on the map and multiplying this number by 10 (since each 10 cm step corresponds to 10 km). In the process of measuring the coastline this way, however, we will have skipped over many details on the map—small bays, inlets, and the like.

To get a more accurate measure of coast length we could use even finer spacing—say 1 cm. Because this finer setting would let us get into some (but not all) of the finer details along the coast, our calculated coast length (given by the number of 1 cm divider steps multiplied by 1) will be longer than our previous value. If we were now to use a more detailed map (one with a scale of 0.1 km per cm, for example), or if we were to use a smaller divider setting, we would pick up even more detail and thus obtain an even larger value for the coast length. In fact, the measured coastline increases as the measuring increment decreases. Imagine measuring around each rock outcropping and sand bank along the coast. This would produce an even longer coast length. And if we were to measure around each grain of sand at the water's edge, the number would be larger still.

And so the answer to the question "How long is the coast of California?" is "It depends."

It depends on what? It depends on the length of the measuring stick used in making the measurement. This is because the use of any measuring stick will result in a smoothing out of details that would have been measured if the stick were smaller.

Disputes on this topic have actually strained relationships between countries with shared borders, although this has become less of an issue.

Aside from being of obvious interest to mapmakers, problems of this sort have led to the creation of a new branch of mathematics called fractal geometry. Although the formal aspects of this geometry have their roots in work performed in the early 1900s, its detailed development resulted from the work of Benoit Mandelbrot in the 1950s. He coined the word fractal in 1975 to denote a mathematical set or concrete object whose form is extremely irregular and/or fragmented at all scales.

Our interest in fractals is twofold. First, many of the fractal curves are beautiful to look at. Second, simple Lynx procedures can be written to describe these curves—curves that defied traditional mathematical analysis and were considered monstrosities by many early twentieth-century mathematicians.

Since many objects in the real world—from coastlines to blood vessels—are more accurately described by fractals than by smooth approximations, this field of mathematics will be receiving even more attention in the future.

Some Simple Fractal Curves

Let's start with a horizontal line one unit long. (The unit might be a kilometer, a centimeter, the length of your finger—it doesn't matter.)

This line represents our first approximation to a coastline we want to measure. Suppose that we now set the dividers to a spacing of 1/3 unit and measure the coast again. We might obtain this result.

This coastline has a triangular bump in it and is made from four lines, each of which is 1/3 unit in length. The total length of the coastline is now 4/3 units.

Suppose that we now reduce the setting of the dividers to 1/3 of the previous setting and measure the coast again. What we discover (for this special coastline) is that each of the 1/3 unit straight lines is actually a replica of the coastline shown in the preceding figure. From this figure, we can see that each of the 1/3 unit lines is made of four lines, just as the preceding figure was. Since our new approximation has increase the length of each line by 4/3 over its previous value, the new length of the coast is 4/3 * 4/3, or 16/9 units long.

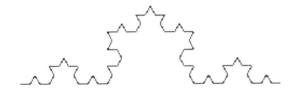

Suppose that we repeat this process again and discover that each of these straight line segments is in fact made from another four segments. This generates a coastline approximation that is 4/3 * 4/3 * 4/3, or 64/27 units long—more than twice our original length.

What we have created is a very strange mathematical figure that has the property of increasing its length by 4/3 each time we reduce the size of our measuring stick by 1/3. If we continue this process indefinitely, we will end up with an infinitely long coastline that is pinned at both ends and around which we could draw a smooth boundary. The American mathematician Norbert

Wiener observed that, even though the length of this curve is infinite, it can be completely enclosed in a sausage-like shape. And, yes, the resulting shape is called a Wiener Sausage.

Our strange figure is, in the limit, both infinitely long and infinitely bumpy. This original shape, called a triadic Koch curve, was discovered by H. von Koch in the early 1900s. Mathematicians of his day generally refused to study such "poorly behaved" functions. As we shall see, however, such functions are very easy to describe when using a computer language that supports recursive procedures.

Explicit Procedures for Drawing Fractals

Before developing a single recursive procedure for drawing approximations to the triadic Koch curve, we will explore some explicit methods that will help us understand the recursive form later.

The first procedures we will create are based on the second figure in this chapter. To draw this figure, we can use the following two procedures:

```
TO K0 :SIZE
FORWARD :SIZE
END

TO K1 :SIZE
K0 :SIZE / 3
LEFT 60
K0 :SIZE / 3
RIGHT 120
K0 :SIZE / 3
LEFT 60 K0
:SIZE / 3
END
```

(This may appear to be a hard way to draw the figure, but the power of this method will become obvious soon.)

To see the result of these procedures, we should start with the turtle near the left edge of the screen and facing to the right. The following setup procedure should do the job nicely:

```
TO SETUP
PENUP SETPOS [-120 -60]
PENDOWN RIGHT 90
END
```

Now enter

```
CG
SETUP
K1 243
```

(We chose 243 for the length of the curve because it fills the screen nicely and because it is a power of 3. The latter characteristic ensures that our more complex renditions of this figure will be drawn with integer line lengths.)

Suppose that we want to draw the next level of this curve. To do this, we need to replace each straight line segment with a replica of the figure generated by K1 with the value of SIZE reduced by a third. The following procedure does this for us:

```
TO K2 :SIZE
K1 :SIZE / 3
LEFT 60
K1 :SIZE / 3
RIGHT 120
K1 :SIZE / 3
LEFT 60
K1 :SIZE / 3
END
```

As you can see, K2 is identical to K1 except that K2 uses the procedure K1 and K1 uses the procedure K0. To see the result of this procedure, enter

```
CG
SETUP
K2 243
```

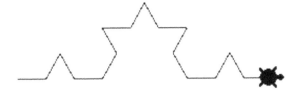

By now, it should be pretty clear that we can generate the next level of the Koch curve by creating the procedure

```
TO K3 :SIZE
K2 :SIZE / 3
LEFT 60
K2 :SIZE / 3
RIGHT 120
K2 :SIZE / 3
LEFT 60
K2 :SIZE / 3
END
```

To see this level of the curve, enter

```
CG
SETUP
K3 243
```

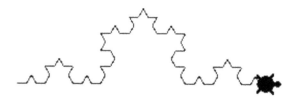

By making a simple modification to K3, we can create the procedure K4, which gives yet another level of detail to our figure. Once you have created K4, you should be able to generate this figure.

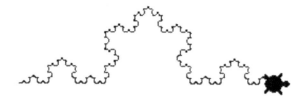

How far do we need to continue this process? We could easily create procedures up to K20 or so, but do we really need to? Since our original procedure, K1, drew lines that were 243/3, or 81 units long, the lines drawn by K2 were 27 units long. K3 used 9 unit lines, K4 used 3 units, and, if we were to define it, K5 would use lines 1 screen unit long. Since the computer's display screen can't handle lines less than 1 unit long, it hardly makes sense to try to create this curve with any more resolution than that.

This does not mean that the fractal curve can be accurately represented by only five levels of complexity. The true fractal triadic Koch curve uses infinitely many levels of procedures.

Because of Lynx's ability to use recursion, we will be able to create a single compact procedure that represents the triadic Koch curve (or any other fractal) to any level of accuracy we wish.

Recursive Procedures for Drawing Fractals

If we look at procedures K0 through K4, we can see a clue that will show us how to create these fractal curves with only one procedure. The first thing to notice is that K0 is the only procedure that actually draws any lines. The other procedures only use lower-numbered procedures or turn the turtle. By writing the actual steps as they are executed, we can show how these procedures work. Let's examine K2, for example. If we expand the steps, we can see the sequence of commands as they are carried out. When we used K2, it used K1 4 times and K1 used K0 16 times to actually draw the lines. Because of the similarities between K1, K2, K3, and so on, we should be able to use one procedure to create Koch curves with any level of complexity we want. We can do this because when Lynx procedures use themselves recursively, Lynx creates as many new copies of the procedure as are needed to keep the levels uniquely identified.

The only procedure we created that is markedly different from the rest is K0, because it only draws lines. The following procedure incorporates all the features of K0, K1, K2, and so on, into one compact form that lets us generate any level of triadic Koch curve we desire:

```
TO TRIAD :SIZE :LIMIT
IF :SIZE < :LIMIT [FORWARD :SIZE STOP]
TRIAD :SIZE / 3 :LIMIT
LEFT 60
TRIAD :SIZE / 3 :LIMIT
RIGHT 120
TRIAD :SIZE / 3 :LIMIT
LEFT 60
TRIAD :SIZE / 3 :LIMIT
 END
```

To see how this procedure operates, let's examine it line by line. Suppose that you gave the command TRIAD 243 100, for example. First, the size (243) would be tested to see if it is less than the limit (100). Because it is not, TRIAD would be used again with a size of 243/3, or 81. Since, in this new use of TRÍAD, the size (81) is less than 100, a line will be drawn (just as with the K0 procedure). As soon as this happens, the STOP command forces Lynx back to the earlier version of TRIAD to carry out its next command (LEFT 60). This process is continued in just the same way that K1 used K0. The only difference is that we are taking advantage of Lynx's ability to keep track of multiple uses of a procedure that we have defined only once. It is as though Lynx makes as many copies of TRIAD as it needs and gives them special names so that they are used in the right order.

The concept of recursive programming is probably the trickiest and most powerful concept you will encounter as you use computers. If you are confused by recursion, you may want to reexamine the previous section before exploring the next examples.

As a measure of recursion's power, notice that TRIAD can be used to describe any level of approximation to the triadic Koch curve. The ten-line procedure is all that is needed to describe a mathematical curve that was avoided by many mathematicians for years!

Experiment with TRIAD (leaving the turtle visible). By watching the figure being drawn, you might gain more insight into the way that recursion is being used to create the figure. To generate the figures we have already drawn, you might use

```
TRIAD 243 243
TRIAD 243 81
TRIAD 243 27
TRIAD 243 9
```

Remember to clear the screen and use SETUP before drawing each curve. To see the most detailed level of this curve that can be shown on the screen, enter

```
CG
SETUP
TRIAD 243 3
```

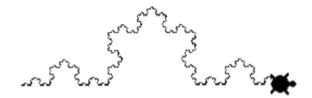

Fractals can be generated from any pattern that can be used in a self-replicating manner. For example, suppose that we use a square-cornered figure instead of the triangular one we used previously.

Since each of the five lines used in this figure is one-third the span of the pattern from left to right, we can generate the next-level curve by repeating this pattern in place of each straight line segment. The following procedure lets us generate this curve to any level complexity we desire:

```
TO QUADRIC :SIZE :LIMIT
IF :SIZE < :LIMIT [FORWARD :SIZE STOP]
QUADRIC :SIZE / 3 :LIMIT
LEFT 90
QUADRIC :SIZE / 3 :LIMIT
RIGHT 90
QUADRIC :SIZE / 3 :LIMIT
RIGHT 90
QUADRIC :SIZE / 3 :LIMIT
LEFT 90
QUADRIC :SIZE / 3 :LIMIT
END
```

To see the patterns that result from this fractal procedure, try these values (remembering to clear the screen and use SETUP before each figure is drawn):

QUADRIC 243 243

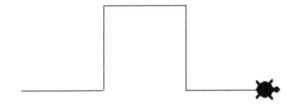

QUADRIC 243 81

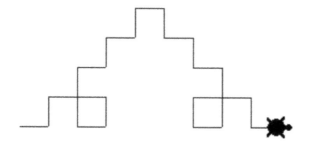

QUADRIC 243 27

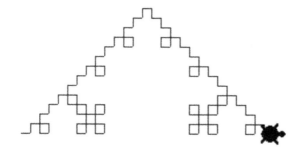

QUADRIC 243 9

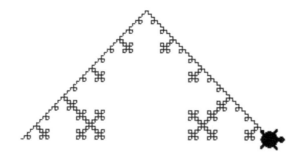

QUADRIC 243 3

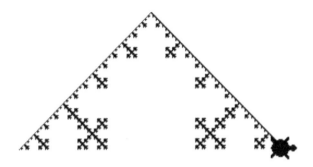

It is interesting that an exploration of the length of a coastline could lead us to a pattern that would look more at home on a lace napkin.

To see a completely closed pattern based on this figure (a quadric Koch island), enter the following procedure:

```
TO ISLAND SIZE :LIMIT
REPEAT 4 [QUADRIC :SIZE :LIMIT RIGHT 90]
END
```

Now you can create a complete closed figure by entering

```
CG PENUP SETPOS [ -20 -30] PENDOWN ISLAND 81 9
```

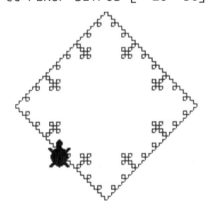

Does it surprise you to know that the turtle's net turning for this figure is 360 degrees?

In the next chapter, we will explore a few more examples of recursive procedures.

12 – Trees and Other Subjects

I think that I shall never see
A procedure lovely as a tree.
But unless I master the recursive call
I'll never see a tree at all.
– Trees and Branching

The types of fractal curves we examined in the last chapter represent only a small sampling of the myriad geometric forms that are built from copies of a master unit. If you examine a tree, for example, you can see a single large trunk that carries several large branches, each of which carries smaller branches, and so on. Finally, from small twigs, we see clusters of leaves. In many ways, this description of a tree suggests that we can use a recursive Lynx procedure to draw them.

Let's start, for example, with a simple forked pattern of new branches that would appear at the end of each older branch. Our challenge is to define a procedure that will create a pattern of branches whose ends each contain the same branching pattern, reduced in size by some factor.

A simple branch pair can be constructed by a simple procedure that leaves the turtle in the same position in which it started:

```
TO BRANCH :SIZE
SETPENSIZE 2
LEFT 45
FORWARD :SIZE
BACK :SIZE
RIGHT 90
FORWARD :SIZE
BACK :SIZE
LEFT 45
END
```

This procedure draws the first branch and then comes back to the origin before drawing the second branch. After the second branch is drawn, the turtle returns to the origin and orients itself to its original position. To replicate this pattern at the end of each branch tip, we need to repeat the branching process when the turtle has reached the end of each previous branch. The following procedure is very similar to BRANCH but contains some important differences:

```
TO TREE :SIZE :LIMIT :TRUNK
IF :SIZE < :LIMIT [STOP]
SETPENSIZE :TRUNK
LEFT 45
FORWARD :SIZE
TREE :SIZE * 0.61803 :LIMIT :TRUNK - 1
BACK :SIZE
SETPENSIZE :TRUNK
RIGHT 90
FORWARD :SIZE
TREE :SIZE * 0.61803 :LIMIT :TRUNK - 1
BACK :SIZE
LEFT 45
END
```

By having the pen size change with each level of recursion, the tree looks more real than if all the branches were the same size. The major differences between TREE and BRANCH are, first, that TREE is used recursively at the end of each branch. The sizes of the recursive branches are each reduced by a factor of 0.61803 from the length of the previous branch. You can use any factor you wish in place of this value. For example, a value of 0.5 will make the new branches half as long as the previous ones. The factor we have chosen (based on the golden mean) makes a very pretty tree (as we shall soon see). The other major difference between TREE and BRANCH is the test to check if :SIZE is less than :LIMIT. This test serves the same purpose it did for our fractal procedures in the last chapter. This type of conditional expression is needed in all recursive procedures of this type.

To generate a display of our simple tree, enter

```
CG
TREE 64 2 6
SETPENSIZE 10
BACK 64
```

As this figure is being drawn, you can see clearly the various levels of recursion being used to generate the tree. The last command (BACK 64) provides our tree with a trunk.

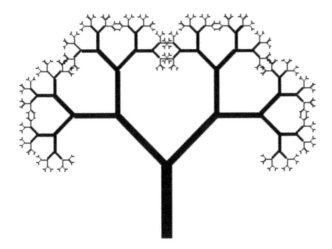

If you study the picture generated by TREE 64 2 closely, you may see a recursive family of hearts formed by the intertwining branches. As pretty as this picture is, it is far too symmetrical to look very realistic. However, one could use this pattern to generate an interesting Valentine picture by entering

CG REPEAT 2 [TREE 64 2 6 RIGHT 180]

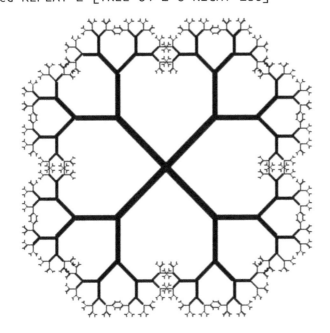

How do we generate a more realistic looking tree? Our first example underwent branching at exactly the same point on both branches. In real trees, this is highly unlikely.

Suppose that we designed a procedure that used a simple two-element branch for which the left arm was twice as long as the right arm. This is still far from realistic, but it gives us an interesting pattern.

Instead of reducing the size of the branches as the tree grows, we can leave them the same size to see what effect this has on the final pattern. An unfortunate consequence of this approach is that we can no longer examine the branch size to determine which level of recursion we are using, so we will use a simple counter for this purpose. Enter the following procedure:

```
TO FTREE :SIZE :COUNTER :TRUNK
IF :COUNTER = 0 [STOP]
SETPENSIZE :TRUNK
LEFT 30
FORWARD :SIZE * 2
FTREE :SIZE :COUNTER - 1 :TRUNK - 1
BACK :SIZE * 2
SETPENSIZE :TRUNK
RIGHT 60
FORWARD :SIZE
FTREE :SIZE :COUNTER - 1 :TRUNK - 1
BACK :SIZE
LEFT 30
END
```

If you trace the operation of this procedure, you can see its similarities to the previous TREE procedure.

To see the pattern generated by this procedure, enter

```
CG PENUP SETY -40 PENDOWN FTREE 20 5 5 SETPENSIZE 7
BACK 40
```

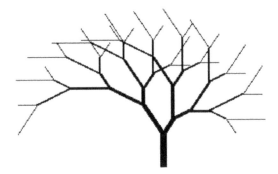

This is a far more realistic looking tree because of its apparent asymmetry. Some branches cross over others, and the tree leans a bit off center—much as a real tree might.

It so happens that this tree has another interesting property. Let us suppose that the growth rate for both branches is the same, so that the longer branch takes twice as long to grow as the shorter one. We can then draw contour lines of equal growth for this tree and count the number of branches crossed by each contour line.

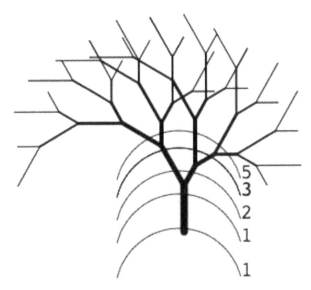

When we do this, we are presented with the series 112358... the Fibonacci series! The procedure FTREE creates a Fibonacci tree. Thus we see yet another example of this series' spontaneous appearance in nature and mathematics.

Random Motions

Thus far, we have presented illustrations that suggest the presence of a tremendous amount of order in the universe. It is only fair that we devote at least some time to chaos, since chaos is the wellspring from which all order arises. Just as Lynx is an appropriate language for the exploration of symmetry, it can let us study randomness as well. The principal tool for this is the operation RANDOM. If you enter the command

```
SHOW RANDOM 100
```

a number between 0 and 99 will be typed on the screen. Each time RANDOM is used, it randomly picks an integer from 0 to one less than the limit specified.

The easiest way to explore random motions is to have the turtle "walk" around the screen in fixed length steps. After each step, the turtle is randomly pointed in another direction.

For example, enter

```
CG ST REPEAT 50 [FORWARD 20 RIGHT RANDOM 360]
```

As you can see, the turtle is buffeted about as it moves. The path it creates is quite confusing. This type of motion is characteristic of small dust particles buffeted by the random motions of air molecules. It is called Brownian motion, after its discoverer.

It is this random motion of molecules that results in the ultimately uniform dispersal of a drop of ink in a glass of water. To see the result of random motion for a particle constrained to be on the display screen, enter

```
CG REPEAT 1000 [FORWARD 10 RIGHT RANDOM 360]
```

As you can see, some areas of the screen are covered quite thoroughly, while others are left open. Yet, if we allowed the process to continue indefinitely, we would find that the turtle was equally likely to have covered any screen location.

One limitation of the fractal coastlines we explored in the preceding chapter is that, like our first tree, they are too symmetrical. Real coastlines (or mountain ranges) appear to be far more random in their appearance.

Whether or not mountain ranges are random is beside the point, however. Their appearance of randomness allows us to create a procedure for drawing mountain ranges.

The randomness of mountain tops is of a special sort. Clearly, the angles of the bumps are not so unconstrained as to make them look like the path of a particle undergoing Brownian motion. Also, the jagged outline of the mountains appears to use sides of varying lengths. This suggests that a procedure for drawing mountain ranges should use two sorts of randomness—a limited randomness in the direction of the drawn line and a limited randomness in the length of the drawn line.

If our mountains were perfectly flat, the turtle's heading would always be 90 degrees. The bumpiness of the mountain range is determined by the extent to which the angles are allowed to vary around this value. The following procedure lets us create mountain ranges with different amounts of bumpiness:

```
TO MOUNTAINS :BUMP
PENUP SETHEADING 90 BACK 120 PENDOWN
REPEAT 60 [SETHEADING ((90 - :BUMP) + RANDOM (2* :BUMP)
) FORWARD RANDOM 15] END
```

These figures were generated with different amounts of bumpiness. (Remember to clear the screen before drawing each mountain range.)

MOUNTAINS 15

MOUNTAINS 30

MOUNTAINS 60

MOUNTAINS 90

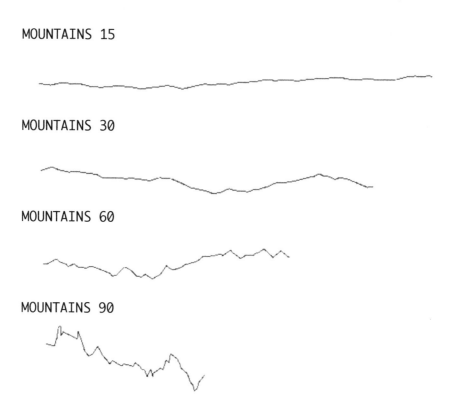

Depending on where you live, you might be able to see a silhouette of mountains on the horizon that appears similar to one of these figures.

The use of random numbers in geometry allows us to create many patterns that closely represent some aspects of the world around us. Harmony coexists with chaos, and mastery of both is essential for even a partial understanding of the universe.

Conclusion – The Tyranny of Space

All patterns, whether drawn by artists, calculated by mathematicians, or produced by natural forces are shaped by the same spatial environment. All are subject to the tyranny of space. Synthetic patterns of lines and dots are engaging in their own right but, more importantly, they speak eloquently of the order that all things inevitably share.
– Peter Stevens, *Patterns in Nature*

There have been several observations made in this book that appear to be universally true. We have seen, for example, that any simple planar closed path results in a total turning angle of 360 degrees. We have seen that the sum of the interior angles around any node of a tessellation must equal 360 degrees. We have seen several examples of the spontaneous appearance of the golden mean.

Yet these observations are only true for the dimensionalities of space in which we exist. But just what is the dimensionality of our space?

We think of ourselves as living in a three-dimensional world—a world in which physical objects have height, breadth, and depth. Because of our comprehension of three-dimensional space, it is easy for us to understand spaces with fewer dimensions (for example, two), but it is harder for us to develop intuitions regarding spaces with more dimensions (for example, four).

Because we think of the three dimensions of our experience as lines, areas, and volumes, one might assume that the only dimensions we have are given by the integers 1, 2, and 3. For example, we can say that a three-dimensional volume is characterized by the fact that if two parallel surfaces are brought arbitrarily close together within this volume, there would be "volume" between the surfaces for any arbitrary separation. Similarly, two parallel one-dimensional lines can be brought arbitrarily close to each other on a two-dimensional surface and there will still be "surface" between them. Finally, two zero-dimensional points can be brought arbitrarily close to each other on a one-dimensional line and there would still be a "line" between them. This model of dimensionality was well known to philosophers such as Aristotle and has profoundly influenced the way we think about our universe. We often think of objects as having surfaces and volumes, and we often talk about connecting points with lines. We must ask, however, if this restriction to integer dimensions (and the corresponding labels of line, surface, and volume) is relevant to the real world. What, for example, is the surface of a sponge? What is its volume? Do we define a sponge's surface as the area of a sheet of smooth material that just covers it? Alternatively, we must examine the surface area of the pores that characterize the sponge's squishiness. If we go too far in that direction, however, we might decide that a sponge is mostly surface, with almost no volume. The trade-off between apparent surface and apparent volume for physical objects like sponges suggests that a mathematical model of a sponge might benefit from the use of other dimensions. As pleasing as the concept of integer dimensions might be (along with the corresponding concepts of line, surface, and volume), we should feel free to broaden our concept of dimension to include dimensions that are nonintegers and that are not pure lines, surfaces, or volumes. Without knowing it, we have already encountered figures with noninteger dimensions—the fractals.

To understand this concept, we must first develop a general expression for dimensionality. This general expression will have the property of being consistent with our intuitions regarding lines, surfaces, and volumes, but will also free us to examine other dimensions.

Consider, first, a one-dimensional straight line of unit length that has been divided into N equal pieces of length r.

We can see that

$N = (1/r)$

As r is decreased, N increases linearly—the expected result for a one-dimensional line.

Next, let us examine a two-dimensional square of 1 unit length that has been divided into N equal subsquares of length r.

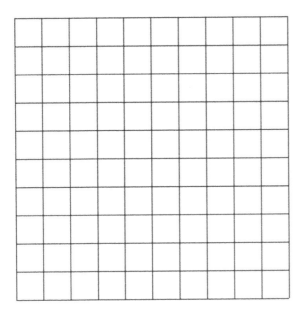

From this figure we can see that

$$N = (1/r)^2$$

As r is decreased, N increases by the second power of $1/r$—the expected result for a two-dimensional figure. You can easily see that a similar result holds true for the cube (using the third power). What we have found is that the exponent of this equation corresponds to the dimension of the object we are dividing into N pieces.

In general, we can state that

$$N = (1/r)^D$$

in which D is the dimensionality of the object under study. By taking the logarithm of both sides of the equation, we find that

$$\log N = D \log (1/r)$$

and, by rearranging the terms, that the dimensionality is given by

$$D = \log N / \log (1/r)$$

Calculated this way, D is called the Hausdorff dimension after Felix Hausdorff, one of the pioneers in the mathematical field of topology.

Now let's apply this result to the two fractal curves we examined in Chapter 11.

The triadic Koch curve is based on this figure.

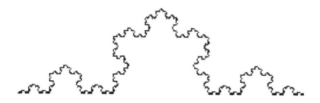

Each time the length of our measuring unit (r) is reduced by a factor of 3, the number of separate segments increases by 4. We can see this by counting the segments for the first few levels of division. We start with 4 segments. When we divide the length by 3, the number of segments increases to 16. When we divide by 3 again, the number increases to 64. If this curve were one-dimensional, then each time we divided it by 3, the number of segments would increase by 3. If it were two-dimensional, then the number of segments would increase by 3 to the second power, or 9. Since the number of segments actually increases by 4, we can begin to develop an intuitive feeling for the idea that this curve has a dimension intermediate between 1 and 2. In fact, for this figure, $N = 4$ and $r = 1/3$. Thus,

$D = \log 4 / \log 3 = 1.2619....$

This curve has a dimensionality somewhere between that of a line and an area. As a result, it is neither a line nor an area, but something else altogether. Because the dimension is fairly close to 1, we might say that this curve is more like a line than it is like an area, but what does that really mean?

The second curve we explored was the quadric fractal based on this figure.

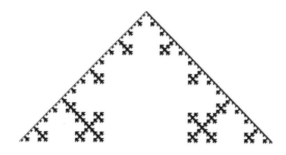

For this figure, a reduction of *r* by 1/3 results in the number of segments increasing by a factor of 5. This curve has a dimension given by

$D = \log 5 / \log 3 = 1.4650. ...$

We can say that this second curve is closer to a two dimensional figure than is the first. This is confirmed by our own observation when the two fractals are compared. The second figure appears to fill more area than the first.

Perhaps one way to further understand the nature of fractional dimensions is to explore a fractal with a dimension of 2. The following procedure generates one example of a two-dimensional fractal:

```
TO TWODIM :SIZE :LIMIT
IF :SIZE < :LIMIT [FORWARD :SIZE STOP]
TWODIM :SIZE / 2 :LIMIT
LEFT 90
TWODIM :SIZE / 2 :LIMIT
RIGHT 180
TWODIM :SIZE / 2 :LIMIT
LEFT 90
TWODIM :SIZE / 2 :LIMIT
END
```

To see the patterns that result from this fractal procedure, try these values (remembering to clear the screen and use the SETUP procedure we defined in Chapter 11 before each figure is drawn):

TWODIM 256 256

TWODIM 256 64

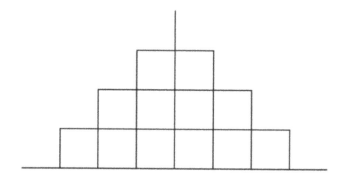

TWODIM 256 16

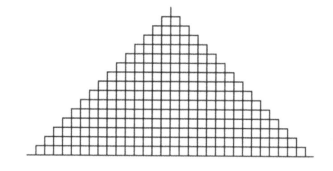

TWODIM 256 4

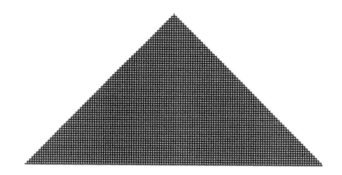

These figures clearly illustrate the emerging transition from a simple set of lines to a completely covered area as the number of segments is allowed to increase.

As each level of the curve is generated, it adds lines between those also generated at earlier levels. Ultimately as the number of segments increases without bound, we achieve complete surface coverage with this fractal.

Perhaps you are beginning to feel more comfortable with the concept of non integer dimensions. It is a concept that is so new and strange that it might take a few weeks for it to make sense to you. As you can see however, our arbitrary restriction of dimensions to the integers is inadequate to describe either nature or certain objects in mathematics.

If space can accommodate fractals, then what about time? Does time have fractal characteristics? Remember that one aspect of fractal figures is that they get longer as our measuring stick gets shorter. Our subjective experience with time is very reminiscent of this. An hour spent at a concert or ball game can seem like a few minutes, but the four minutes spent watching a clock while taking a child's temperature can seem like an hour. Our subjective exposure to the fractal aspects of time is well expressed by the saying "A watched pot never boils."

Each of us has a lifetime of experience with subjective time intervals. Some short events take forever (it seems), and some long events are over too soon. Our use of mechanical time-measuring devices gives an order to our existence that would be missing if we each operated on our own time scheme. Even before the invention of the clock, we used the sun, moon, seasons, and stars to provide us with measures of days, months, quarters, and years. But suppose that we had no clocks, and suppose that we were fixed in space along with the sun, moon, and stars. What would time be for us then? Perhaps the rhythm of our heartbeats and breathing would provide us with another system for measuring time. Would the short intervals of these events cause us to think of time as "taking longer"?

As with so many aspects of the universe in which we live, there are no easy answers to these questions. Perhaps it is enough to be able to ask the questions and to speculate on their answers. That has been one of the goals of this book—and it is one of the appropriate uses of Lynx.

I have chosen to call this chapter a conclusion, but it is far from that. Some of the subjects we have introduced have enchanted people for millennia, and they promise to do so for thousands of years to come.

If some of these topics have stimulated your interest in pattern and mathematics, then you are on the path to making your own discoveries of beauty.

Also from Constructing Modern Knowledge Press

Visit CMKPress.com for more information

Invent to Learn: Making, Tinkering, and Engineering in the Classroom

by Sylvia Libow Martinez and Gary S. Stager
An all new and expanded edition of the book called "the bible of the Maker Movement in classrooms," *Invent To Learn* has become the most popular book for educators seeking to understand how modern tools and technology can revolutionize education.

The Art of Digital Fabrication: STEAM Projects for the Makerspace and Art Studio

by Erin E. Riley

Integrate STEAM in your school through arts-based maker projects using digital fabrication tools commonly found in makerspaces like 3D printers, laser cutters, vinyl cutters, and CNC machines. Full color pages showcase the artistic and technical work of students that results from combining art with engineering and design. Written by an educator with experience in art and maker education, this volume contains over twenty-five makerspace tested projects, a material and process inventory for digital fabrication, guides for designing with software, and how-tos for using digital fabrication machines.

Scrappy Circuits

by Michael Carroll

The best dollar you'll ever spend on a child's STEAM education! Scrappy Circuits is an imaginative "do-it-yourself" way to learn about electrical circuits for less than $1 per person. Raid your junk drawer for simple office supplies, add a little cardboard, pay a visit to a local dollar store, and you are on your way to countless fun projects for learning about electronics.

The Invent to Learn Guide to Fun

by Josh Burker

The Invent to Learn Guide to Fun features an assortment of insanely clever classroom-tested maker projects for learners of all ages. Josh Burker kicks classroom learning-by-making up a notch with step-by-step instructions, full-color photos, open-ended challenges, and sample code. Learn to paint with light, make your own Operation Game, sew interactive stuffed creatures, build Rube Goldberg machines, design artbots, produce mathematically generated mosaic tiles, program adventure games, and more!

The Invent to Learn Guide to MORE Fun

by Josh Burker

Josh Burker is back with a second volume of all new projects for learners who just want MORE! Insanely clever classroom-tested "maker" projects for learners of all ages with coding, microcontrollers, 3D printing, LEGO machines, and more! The projects feature step-by-step instructions and full-color photos.

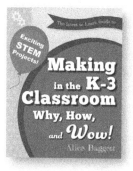

The Invent to Learn Guide to Making in the K-3 Classroom: Why, How, and Wow!

by Alice Baggett

This full color book packed with photos is a practical guide for primary school educators who want to inspire their students to embrace a tinkering mindset so they can invent fantastic contraptions. Veteran teacher Alice Baggett shares her expertise in how to create hands-on learning experiences for young inventors so students experience the thrilling process of making—complete with epic fails and spectacular discoveries.

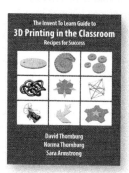

The Invent to Learn Guide to 3D Printing in the Classroom: Recipes for Success

by David Thornburg, Norma Thornburg, and Sara Armstrong

This book is an essential guide for educators interested in bringing the amazing world of 3D printing to their classrooms. Eighteen fun and challenging projects explore science, technology, engineering, and mathematics, along with forays into the visual arts and design.

Meaningful Making: Projects and Inspirations for Fab Labs & Makerspaces (Volumes 1 & 2)

Edited by Paulo Blikstein, Sylvia Libow Martinez, Heather Allen Pang

Project ideas, articles, best practices, and assessment strategies from educators at the forefront of making and hands-on, minds-on education. In these two volumes, FabLearn Fellows share inspirational ideas from their learning spaces, assessment strategies and recommended projects across a broad range of age levels. Illustrated with color photos of real student work, the Fellows take you on a tour of the future of learning, where children make sense of the world by making things that matter to them and their communities.

Making Science: Reimagining STEM Education in Middle School and Beyond

by Christa Flores

Anthropologist turned science and making teacher Christa Flores shares her classroom tested lessons and resources for learning by making and design in the middle grades and beyond. Richly illustrated with examples of student work, this book offers project ideas, connections to the Next Generation Science Standards, assessment strategies, and practical tips for educators.

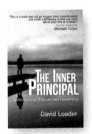

The Inner Principal: Reflections on Educational Leadership

by David Loader

"This is a book that will go to your inner consciousness and make a difference in how you think about your own role as leader." – from the foreword by Michael Fullan

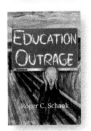

Education Outrage

by Roger C. Schank

Roger Schank has had it with the stupid, lazy, greedy, cynical, and uninformed forces setting outrageous education policy, wrecking childhood, and preparing students for a world that will never exist. The short essays in this book will make you mad, sad, argue with your friends, and take action.